CONSTITUTIONAL ANALYSIS
IN A
NUTSHELL

By

JERRE S. WILLIAMS
Professor of Law
University of Texas School of Law

ST. PAUL, MINN.
WEST PUBLISHING CO.
1979

Nu'shell Series, In a Nutshell, the Nutshell Logo and the WP symbol are registered trademarks of West Publishing Co. Registered in U.S. Patent and Trademark Office.

COPYRIGHT © 1979 By WEST PUBLISHING CO.

Printed in the United States of America

Library of Congress Cataloging in Publication Data

Williams, Jerre Stockton, 1916–
    Constitutional analysis in a nutshell.

    (Nutshell series)
    Includes index.
    1. United States—Constitutional law. I. Title.
KF4550.Z9W53   342'.73'02   78–23987

ISBN 0–8299–2022–6

TEXT IS PRINTED ON 10% POST CONSUMER RECYCLED PAPER

PRINTED WITH SOY INK™

Williams—Const.Analysis
5th Reprint—1995

To
Judge Mary Pearl Williams
and to
Stockton, lawyer
and
Shelley and Stephanie, soon to be lawyers

*

FOREWORD

This book is based upon over thirty years of experience in teaching constitutional analysis to law students. It is not intended to be a comprehensive text of constitutional law in the United States. It is, instead, a framework for constitutional analysis.

More than 4,000 lawyers who have been exposed to this analysis directly in class as law students would recognize it immediately. It is gratifying for me to recall the number of times former students have told me the analysis here presented stuck firmly in their minds and proved to be useful and effective in cases in which they were later involved.

The decision to put this analysis in a separate small volume arose only recently. It is incorporated in a much longer manuscript which I have been working on for several years, a text and critique of the work of the Supreme Court in interpreting the Constitution. But in the summer of 1977, I had the opportunity to teach Comparative Civil Rights—United Kingdom and United States, to a group of American law students at Merton College, Oxford, under the sponsorship of the Comparative Law Program of the University of San Diego Law School. A number of members of that class had just completed regular courses in

Constitutional Law at law schools in the United States. During the course, several of them indicated they felt the analysis now presented in this book was exceedingly helpful to them. One student, editor-in-chief of her school's law review, particularly urged that the analysis be published. She reported she had gotten a high grade in her Constitutional Law course, but she felt she had never really understood it until she participated in the Comparative Civil Rights course. It was the experience of the summer of 1977 which led to the writing of this manuscript.

In addition to being useful to law students and lawyers, it is my hope that this book can be useful to intelligent laymen who are interested in the work of the Supreme Court in "declaring statutes unconstitutional." A framework is presented to aid in understanding how constitutional liberty as it relates to governmental power is manifested in our system through the outstandingly important role played by the United States Supreme Court.

Appendix B is the text of the U. S. Constitution. It is not relegated to the last place in the book to suggest less importance. Making it Appendix B makes it easier to locate for frequent reference as the book is read.

Appendix A presents a "Leading Case Outline of Constitutional Law." It is included since this book is not a general text of constitutional law. But in building an analytical framework, a basic outline of the substance of constitutional law is a needed and useful reference. So it is included for this purpose. It is not intended to be highly detailed. Its role is to give an overall brief outline of the body of constitutional law.

I want to acknowledge particularly the highly competent and effective editorial assistance of my daughter, Shelley Williams, a second-year student at the University of Texas Law School. And I also acknowledge my appreciation for the outstanding professional level of secretarial and administrative assistance by my longtime secretary, Shirley Green.

JERRE S. WILLIAMS

Austin, Texas
October, 1978

*

OUTLINE

OUTLINE

OUTLINE

OUTLINE

TABLE OF CASES

References are to Pages

TABLE OF CASES

XVI

TABLE OF CASES

TABLE OF CASES

CONSTITUTIONAL ANALYSIS

CHAPTER 1

JUDICIAL REVIEW

1. The Origins of Judicial Review

The Supreme Court of the United States is the most powerful judicial body in the world. The manifestation of this power is the doctrine of "judicial review." The phrase "judicial review" is a shorthand expression for the role the Court plays as the final authority on most, although not all, issues of the constitutionality of governmental acts. It "reviews" these acts to see that they conform to the Constitution. The Court engages not only in judicial review of the constitutionality of legislation, both state and federal, but also of the actions of chief executives, state and federal, as well as decisions of other courts, both state and federal.

The institution of judicial review is so deeply engrained in the American system that it is difficult for us to conceive of a free legal system that does not have it. Our federal and state governmental powers are limited by the Constitution for the purpose of preserving individual liberty, and federal powers are limited to preserve the powers of state governments. The Supreme Court exercises the ultimate authority in enforcing these limitations. Yet the concept of judicial review is a unique American invention. It is fair to say we developed the principle of judicial review out of the common law of England. Although England has a similar history, governmental philosophy, and governmental institutions, it did not develop a concept of judicial review.

The Constitution does not provide specifically for the exercise of judicial review by the Supreme Court. Whether or not the power is implied by language of the Constitution is in dispute among constitutional scholars. But the doctrine did not spring suddenly and spontaneously from unknown origins. It has well-defined ancestry.

The concept of judicial review grows out of three themes found in the common law in England and our law in the United States. The first theme is the concept of "divine law," which later became "natural law" to those who did not demand divinity in the law. This concept of law—that there is divinely ordained law higher than man-made law—is familiar to all persons. It is manifested in the Ten Commandments and other basic rules of human conduct found in other religions or ethical systems. These fundamental tenets, whether "divine" or "natural," have been viewed in our history as "higher law" than the temporal or secular law which governs everyday life.

The second fundamental theme is the principle of "due process of law," which has its beginnings in Magna Carta in 1215. The catch phrase "due process of law," now broadly used in constitutional law as a shorthand description for various procedural and substantive aspects of liberty, developed from the phrase "law of the land," found in Section 39 of the Magna Carta. Its use in the Magna Carta was the means of expressing the then-radical principle that even the king was bound by the "law of the land."

The third paralleling theme was the developing concept that the fundamental law which controls the organization of government should be in writing. The British Parliament, in 1689, enacted the British "Bill of Rights." At the same time, Thomas Hobbes and John Locke were advancing the philosophical concept of the social compact. In their theories the natural law was converted to the concept of natural rights. Men and women lived in a state of nature, and they organized governments only for the purpose of protecting themselves in their freedoms. Thus, government was limited; and it was limited by the social compact, the agreement between the citizens and their government. While the social compact was not originally envisioned as having necessarily to be in writing, the idea that basic liberties must be stated for purposes of protection was unavoidable.

A more explicit fruition of this third theme was occurring at the same time in the colonies. The acceptance of the need for a written constitution derived in part from the colonial charters. The charters were the organic written principles of government of the charter colonies. They were detailed, and they were readily viewed as statements of the fundamental law controlling the operation of the colonies. These charters of government ultimately were developed into state constitutions before the adoption of the United States Constitution. Some of these state constitutions even contained specific provisions for judicial review of the acts of state legislative bodies.

These lines of development were made the basis of the creation of our nation by Thomas Jefferson in the famous words of the Declaration of Independence:

> "We hold these truths to be self-evident, that all men are created equal, that they are endowed by their Creator with certain unalienable Rights, that among these are Life,

Liberty and the pursuit of Happiness—That to secure these Rights, Governments are instituted among Men, deriving their just powers from the consent of the governed * * *."

There remained the issue: Who in our governmental structure would define and enforce our fundamental rights. In the Constitutional Convention the concept of judicial review was discussed, but the Constitution itself contains no words which could be taken as stating clearly and unequivocally that this power to declare laws unconstitutional would exist in the newly created United States Supreme Court.

Yet there was one important basic constitutional document which clearly recognized the power of judicial review before the principle was established by the Supreme Court. This was Federalist Paper No. 78, written by Alexander Hamilton as part of the series of papers undertaking to persuade the states to ratify the newly drafted Constitution. Hamilton set forth the principle of judicial review in unwavering terms. In his discussion, he even presented some of the reasoning which was later used by the Supreme Court in the decision establishing the principle. This is the case set out in the following paragraph.

All of these developments came together in the great case of Marbury v. Madison, 5 U.S. 137

(1 Cranch) in 1803. This is the most important case in all of constitutional law because it established the doctrine of judicial review as a core
legal principle in our constitutional system. The
Supreme Court, in the famous opinion by Chief
Justice Marshall, held unconstitutional a provision of the Judiciary Act of 1789 on the ground
that it attempted to give original jurisdiction to
the United States Supreme Court in a case where
the Constitution limited the Supreme Court's
power to appellate jurisdiction only. The remarkable irony of this decision was that the
Court established its great power of judicial review by holding unconstitutional a statute of
Congress which attempted to give the Court more
power—power to hear certain kinds of cases
which the Court held the Constitution would not
allow.

Actually, there was nothing controversial about
the Judiciary Act. It had been written by Senator Oliver Ellsworth of Connecticut, a distinguished constitutional lawyer who was Marshall's
immediate predecessor as Chief Justice. The
statute's wording was somewhat ambiguous, but
if the same issue were presented today, we would
confidently expect the Court to interpret the statutory words to avoid conflict with the Constitution.

Chief Justice Marshall's reasoning in his opinion was meticulous and detailed. He found the authority for the concept of judicial review lodged largely in two constitutional provisions. Article III sets up the judicial structure of the federal government, and the second clause of Article VI establishes the principle of the supremacy of the United States Constitution. The key words relied upon by the Court were the words of Article III, Section 2: "The Judicial Power shall extend to all Cases, in Law and Equity, arising under this Constitution, * * *." The case of Marbury v. Madison was a "case * * * arising under the Constitution," and the Constitution provides that "*all*" such cases are within the judicial power of the federal government.

Shortly after this decision, other cases made the dominance of the Supreme Court in constitutional matters complete. Acts of state legislatures were declared unconstitutional, Fletcher v. Peck, 10 U.S. (6 Cranch) 87 (1810), and decisions of state courts were declared subject to review by the Supreme Court on a constitutional basis, Martin v. Hunter's Lessee, 14 U.S. (1 Wheat.) 304 (1816).

The recent experience of the Court in dealing with the defiance by state officials of the Court's orders concerning racial integration in the public schools is probably the best example of the scope and strength of the judicial review doctrine. In constitutional terms the culmination of the Supreme Court's position was stated in the critical case of Cooper v. Aaron, 358 U.S. 1, decided in 1958. The decision grew out of defiance by the Governor of Arkansas of the federal court order integrating Central High School in Little Rock. In an act without precedent, the unanimous opinion of the Supreme Court was signed by each of the nine justices by name. The opinion, by way of confirming the earlier school integration decision, Brown v. Board of Education, 347 U.S. 483 (1954), said: "No state legislator or executive or judicial officer can war against the Constitution without violating his undertaking to support it. * * * " 358 U.S. at 18.

2. The Requirement That There be a Case

This brief historical survey of the development of the doctrine of judicial review leads us to consideration of the circumstances under which constitutional questions can be brought to the United States Supreme Court and decided there.

The first and critical requirement is that there must be a *"case."* The Court does not decide questions of constitutionality in abstract or hypothetical situations. It insists that an actual case involving someone who will be hurt by the law or by other governmental action must be submitted to the courts.

The Court has generally defined a case to be a court proceeding which is a bona fide adversary situation where valuable legal rights are being threatened by the action taken, and the Court has the authority and power to resolve the dispute. Fictitious or friendly suits are not acceptable. The parties must be genuinely adversary; someone must be "hurting" from the governmental action. It is by this means that the constitutional issues are made clear and are sharpened.

This requirement that there actually be a flesh-and-blood controversy involving real people caught in a real situation is essential to the understanding of what the Court is doing when it decides issues of constitutionality. Simple examples confirm the need for actual cases adequately to pose constitutional issues. Many constitutional lines depend upon the specific facts and circumstances of the case. In determining the scope of power of the national government to control matters in "interstate commerce," the Court has held that the federal power extends to all of those matters which "affect" interstate commerce. Determination of what "affects" interstate commerce depends inevitably upon the actual factual situations.

Similarly, actual cases are necessary to the effective constitutional evaluation of statutes controlling subversive speech. It would be totally unrealistic to try to decide the constitutionality of a statute without having before the Court the actual words uttered by the person accused of subversive speech. We must see whether the words were prohibited by the statute and whether they were of such danger to our governmental system that we have the right to prohibit them in spite of the protections of free speech contained in the First Amendment.

A third typical example involves the mundane matter of controlling meetings in public parks through the issuance of permits. Such meetings, of course, involve issues of freedom of speech and assembly. Suppose that the public authorities refuse to issue a permit for a particular meeting. What is the nature of the meeting? Are other similar organizations allowed to hold meetings in the park? Is there any substantial danger that the meeting will erupt in violence? Are there any serious problems of littering or damage to the public property in the park? All of these issues are relevant to the critical determination of the constitutionality of denying the right to hold a particular meeting in a public park. These issues cannot be resolved as an abstraction.

The requirement, then, is that to challenge constitutionality you must become involved in a lawsuit. You must sue someone or you must be the subject of someone else's lawsuit. The lawsuit can originate either in a state or federal court, and can be either a criminal case or a suit between private parties. One of the common and best known ways to challenge the constitutionality of regulatory legislation is to violate it for the purpose of creating a constitutional test. The fact that it is a test case does not in any sense lessen its genuineness. The individual making the challenge will suffer the consequences if his or her challenge is unsuccessful. In these more modern days of effective procedures, constitutionality is often challenged by a suit for an injunction to halt enforcement of a regulatory statute.

3. Standing and Ripeness

The Supreme Court has undertaken to insure that the cases which it decides involve real parties and actual intrusion upon legal rights also by establishing the requirements of "standing" and "ripeness." Standing is the broader and more important of the two.

The requirement of standing in the party raising the constitutional issue is actually the requirement that the party himself or herself have a stake in the outcome of the case. Return again to the simple situation of a requirement in a municipal ordinance that permission must be obtained to hold a meeting in a public park. Suppose we have a well-meaning citizen who feels that meetings should be allowed in public parks without restriction. But this citizen is not planning a meeting in the public park, has never attended a meeting in the public park, and indeed never uses or has used or intends to use that public park for any purpose. This citizen is simply someone who believes that the ordinance is unconstitutional. The citizen has no "standing" to raise the constitutional issue concerning the granting of permits for meetings in that public park. The citizen has shown no reason why he or she should be allowed to raise this question. It is simply an abstract question to this particular person, although it would not be abstract to someone who had been denied a permit for a meeting.

A troublesome question involving the right of the individual to raise constitutional issues is whether a taxpayer has the right to challenge how tax money is spent by the government. Does the fact that the taxpayer contributed to the Treasury from which the money for the spending emanates give standing to challenge the spending?

The basic position of the Supreme Court is found in Frothingham v. Mellon, 262 U.S. 447 (1923). It holds that the taxpayer may not challenge general spending from the U. S. Treasury. The interest of a single taxpayer is too small to give standing to challenge federal expenditures. If Mrs. Frothingham's case had gone the other way, every taxpayer would have been entitled to raise the constitutional issue of every instance of federal spending, no matter how minute because of every cent which the federal government spends must have constitutional authorization.

The *Frothingham* holding did raise the spectre of widespread, unconstitutional governmental spending which could never be stopped by the Court because no one would have standing to raise the constitutional issues. But those who were concerned by this possibility overlooked a highly pragmatic consideration. The Supreme Court simply could not afford to get itself in the position of refusing to allow such a critical constitutional issue to be raised.

So it was that when the federal Elementary and Secondary Education Act of 1965 provided for some federal financial aid to private religious schools, the issue was raised of unconstitutional spending of federal funds as a violation of the First Amendment prohibition concerning the establishment of religion. In the 1968 case of Flast

v. Cohen, 392 U.S. 83, the Supreme Court found
the way to allow the taxpayer to challenge these
expenditures. The Court held that the expenditures in this case were not just an instance of a
general authorization of the federal government
to spend funds. This was a situation where the
government spending was alleged to be violating
another specific provision of the Constitution.
Under these circumstances, said the Court, the
taxpayer may challenge the spending even though
the injury is small.

This is a sensible decision. It is the kind of
distinction that the Supreme Court has made
throughout its history in interpreting and applying the Constitution. When the question is a
critical one, in which particular and specific constitutional rights may be violated, and the only
person who can raise the issue is a taxpayer,
standing as a taxpayer should be and is enough.

The Court emphasized that it would not allow a
taxpayer to bring suit to challenge the constitutionality of the spending of governmental funds
in every case which involved a governmental regulatory program. This was a realistic conclusion
because, if a regulatory program is involved,
someone who is being regulated would be more
clearly and specifically hurt by the regulation
than would the taxpayer, and the one regulated

would be entitled, therefore, to raise the constitutional issue.

In addition to the requirement that there be standing to raise the constitutional issue, the Court insists that the issue be "ripe" for judicial decision. An example of the operation of this requirement is found in the 1947 case of United Public Workers v. Mitchell, 330 U.S. 75. This case was an attack upon the Hatch Act ban on partisan political activities by federal employees. The Court held that federal employees who claimed only that they planned to engage in various types of political activity in the future did not present an issue which was ripe for constitutional decision. They had not yet undertaken to do these things but were simply thinking about doing them, so they had not yet been threatened with being hurt by the statute.

The political employees involved were the ones who ultimately were going to be hurt by the statute, and they were planning activities which would bring them into violation of the statute. It can be said, therefore, that they were proper persons to have standing since their legal rights were threatened. But they had not gone far enough in their planning or activities to make the issue one which should be decided now. So the constitutional issues had not matured; they were not yet ripe.

Fortunately to the purpose of resolving the issues involved in the constitutionality of the Hatch Act, one of the government employees bringing the suit had actually engaged in some of the conduct which violated the statute. So as to that employee, the case clearly was "ripe," and the Court did consider the merits of the statute as it applied to this government employee.

A simple description of the requirements of standing and ripeness is found in the words of Justice Stone in the case of Nashville, C. & St. L. Ry. v. Wallace, 288 U.S. 249 (1933). In that opinion, he referred to "valuable legal rights * * * threatened with imminent invasion." The valuable legal rights constitute the standing and the threat of *imminent* invasion constitutes the ripeness.

4. The Forms of Judicial Review

Constitutional challenges rarely begin at lofty levels of great private entities grappling with great governmental power. The case undoubtedly most important in refashioning and remaking our society in recent years involved an 11-year-old black school girl named Linda Brown in Topeka, Kansas, who, with her parents, brought suit protesting the legal requirement in that city that she had to attend a separate school for blacks. This is the case of Brown v. Board of Education of Topeka, 347 U.S. 483, 349 U.S. 294, the basic school integration decision of 1954 and 1955.

Constitutionality may be challenged as the result of police action in breaking up a student demonstration, or labor picketing, or persons parading on a city street. A policeman may challenge the constitutionality of his discharge for alleged improper conduct—perhaps even because his hair was considered to be too long. To state a contrast: a private citizen may protest the payment of a small state tax on goods he received through the mails from another state, or a pregnant woman may demand the right to an abortion. A prisoner in the penitentiary may write his own petition claiming that there was a lack of fairness in the trial in which he was convicted. Such are the seeds of constitutional litigation.

Cases can be filed directly in the United States Supreme Court only in the most limited circumstances—U. S. Constitution, Article III, Section 2, Clause 2. The most common case filed in the Supreme Court is a case in which a state itself is a party and wishes to have its legal rights determined. This kind of case often arises in boundary disputes between states or suits involving state water rights in interstate rivers.

The typical constitutional issues arise in cases brought in federal and state trial courts throughout the nation. Once the case involving the constitutional issue begins, it goes its way through the courts as other cases do. There is trial, decision, and appeal. There is no guarantee that, because a particular case involves a constitutional issue, it will get to the United States Supreme Court. Our highest Court has a limited jurisdiction and in most instances has discretion as to whether it will hear a case.

Cases go to the United States Supreme Court from either a lower federal court or the highest court of the state, usually called a supreme court, but sometimes called a court of appeal. If under state procedure the case is not within the jurisdiction of the highest state court but contains a constitutional issue, it can go directly to the U. S. Supreme Court from the lower state court.

There are three procedures under which a case may move from a lower court to the United States Supreme Court. One of these—"certification"—is a technical procedure under which a lower court, federal only, can state a particular legal issue and ask the Supreme Court for a decision concerning it. The Supreme Court can then either answer the question or call the entire case up for review. This is a procedure which is rarely used and need not be mentioned further because the Court wants the guidance of a decision by the lower federal court and also usually wants to have the entire case before it.

[18]

The two other procedures are the means by which virtually all cases reach the Supreme Court from lower state and federal courts. The first of these procedures is the "appeal," using the word in its narrow technical sense, and the second is by the Court "granting a writ of certiorari," which the litigant has asked the Court to grant. The distinction between these two procedures is that if a party has the right to "appeal" a decision to the Supreme Court, he or she has the right to force the Court to decide the case on the merits. There are narrow exceptions to this right in that the Court may decide the case is so confused that the constitutional issue is not well raised, or the Court may decide that the decision on the case is so obvious that all the Court needs to do is simply to dismiss the appeal. But the statutory provision is a straightforward requirement that the appeal is a matter of right. The Court generally must hear the case.

The compulsory jurisdiction of the Court by way of appeal is stringently limited. If this were not so, the Court would be so loaded down with compulsory cases that it could not handle its entire docket effectively. Constitutional cases are not the Supreme Court's sole concern. A major aspect of its work is the interpretation and application of congressional statutes, often when there is no issue as to constitutionality. In addition, the Court reviews governmental administrative action to insure that statutory requirements have been met, and it reviews federal criminal cases to insure that federal procedural requirements have been carried out. These kinds of cases constitute major portions of the business of the Supreme Court.

There are only two narrow situations in which appeal as a matter of right is the proper procedure to move a case from the state courts to the United States Supreme Court. These two situations are: (1) where the state court has upheld the constitutionality of a state statute as against the claim that it violates the United States Constitution or federal law or treaty, and (2) where the state court has declared unconstitutional a federal statute or treaty. Comparably, there is only one situation where the appeal as a matter of right is authorized procedure to take a case from a federal Court of Appeals to the United States Supreme Court. This is the situation where the federal court has declared a state statute unconstitutional under a claim that it violates the United States Constitution or has declared it is in conflict with federal law or treaty.

The establishment by congressional law of compulsory jurisdiction in the Supreme Court in these narrow situations has firm logical foundation. The logic flows from the delicate relationship between state and federal governments in our system. Thus, the only two situations where there is the right to appeal to the Supreme Court from state courts are the situations in which the state court has upheld a state statute against federal constitutional or legal claim or has struck down a federal statute. These are both situations in which the federal-state relationship demands ultimate decision of these cases by the Supreme Court to protect federal interests. By the same reasoning, the only situation for the right of appeal from the federal Court of Appeals is the one in which the federal court has struck down a state statute as invalid. This protects state interests in our federal system since a federal court has acted against the state.

In contrast to appeals, the majority of cases reaching the Supreme Court are there only because the Court in its discretion granted a petition for a writ of certiorari. In this discretionary area only a very small percentage of cases which the Court is asked to review are ever heard on the merits. In most cases the Court simply denies the petition, allowing the lower court decision to stand as the final decision in the case.

The Court constantly admonishes those who observe its activities that the denial of the review of a case in these discretionary (certiorari) situations is not an indication that the Court agrees with the lower court decision. The Court may be deciding that the case is not worth considering, because it is not important enough, the issues are not posed in effective fashion, there are other less critical issues which confuse the constitutional issue, or similar cases have already been decided.

The Court exercises its discretion in deciding whether it will grant a petition for certiorari under a "rule of four." This simply means that four justices must vote to grant the petition for a writ of certiorari, or the Court will not hear the case. A peculiar anomaly in the Court's procedures is the fact that appeals, although mandatory, are also controlled by the same rule of four votes to review. In appeals, however, the justices are voting first on whether the case is a proper one for appeal. If the case is proper for appeal, then the vote disposing of the case summarily by affirmance or reversal is a vote on the merits. So, if less than four justices vote to hear the appeal, and the case is a proper one for appeal, then the Court is deciding on the merits that the lower court decision is correct.

5. Disposition of a Case on Nonconstitutional Grounds

The requirements to reach the Supreme Court on a constitutional issue having been met, there are still some possible obstacles to authoritative constitutional decision. Two such obstacles deserve only brief mention but two others will then be set out in more detail. There is, first, a procedural requirement insisted upon by the Court that the constitutional issues must be raised as soon as they arise in the case, typically at the trial stage, and raised again at each level throughout the movement of the case through the courts. The purpose of this requirement is to insure that the lower courts have the opportunity to consider the constitutional issue and reach a decision concerning it. It is a matter of deference to the lower courts.

Second, the Court will not consider a constitutional issue if the case has been disposed of in the lower court on some other ground which will justify the decision. If the Court finds that there is an "independent ground" in the state law upon which the court relied for its decision, in addition to its reliance upon the federal constitutional issue, the Court will refuse to consider the constitutional issue. Resolution of the issue would make no difference in the disposition of the case. These are the two relatively narrow procedural matters.

The third means by which the Court may avoid deciding a constitutional issue is the first of the two important ones. This means is generally known and can be described as "interpreting a statute to make it constitutional." This is a common device in the courts. Assume that a statute is ambiguous, as they nearly always are. A broader interpretation would make it unconstitutional, but a narrower interpretation would enable it to be constitutionally acceptable. It is obviously better for the administration of justice to make the narrower interpretation where reasonable. The Court should not go out of its way to declare statutes unconstitutional. It should not assume that the legislative body tried to pass a statute which would be unconstitutional rather than one which would pass constitutional muster.

This mechanism of interpreting statutes to make them constitutional is commonly used by the federal courts with regard to federal statutes and by the high courts of the states concerning their own state statutes.

There is, however, one exceedingly important limitation on this judicial technique which is little known generally and has occasioned much criticism of the Supreme Court. It is an inexorable principle that the Supreme Court may use this technique only with respect to *federal* statutes. It cannot interpret state and local statutes to make them constitutional. This means that the Court must accept the state statute as it has been interpreted by the state court. The Supreme Court is not at liberty to narrow it down to make it constitutional. In turn, this results in decisions by the Supreme Court declaring state statutes and city ordinances unconstitutional in many situations in which, if the statute were federal, the laws would not be declared unconstitutional but would simply be narrowed by interpretation. Since any determination by the Supreme Court that a state or local law is unconstitutional is highly upsetting to state or local governments, these decisions do engender strong criticism of the Court.

The reason for this unwavering principle is that under the federal system the state must be the final authority on the meaning of its own laws. There is no provision in the Constitution giving the federal government power to tell a state what its law is. So the United States Supreme Court has no authority whatsoever to alter the definitive interpretation of state law by a state high court. It may only evaluate its constitutionality as it has been interpreted by the state court.

The temptations are very strong upon the highest state court to give a broad interpretation of a state statute in accordance with the probable intent of the state legislature in the hope that it may withstand constitutional challenge. There is no way that the state court can get clear and controlling guidance as to constitutionality. It can only make its own prediction based upon past Supreme Court decisions. The state court cannot possibly have the insight always to be right on how broad an interpretation the Supreme Court will accept. After all, most constitutional decisions of the Supreme Court find that members themselves split. So there are many instances where the state statutes fall as being unconstitutional when they could have been properly narrowed by interpretation if the state court had known a broader interpretation would be held unconstitutional.

This is in some ways a peculiar and radical doctrine—the highest court of the state is *the final authority* on the interpretation and application of state laws. Its extreme manifestation is seen in the cases where the validity and meaning of state laws sometimes comes into issue in the federal courts. A state statute which has not been interpreted by a state supreme court may be involved in a case which arises in a federal court merely because the plaintiff and defendant are citizens of different states. The Court has jurisdiction in such a case based upon "diversity of citizenship." This jurisdiction is specifically provided for in Article III, Section 2, of the Constitution. So a case in a federal court may have as its only issue the application of a state statute which has not yet been interpreted by the state court. Obviously, the federal court has the obligation to interpret the state statute since it has jurisdiction and must decide the case. But here is the radical idea: the interpretation of the state statute in such a case by the Supreme Court or lower federal court is tentative only. The interpretation given is subject to being "overruled" by the highest court of the state when the statute is called into question in another case.

To make this point totally clear, let it be stated once again: *the final authority* on the interpretation and application of state or local law is the highest court of the state. This principle means that the United States Supreme Court may not use the technique of interpreting a statute to make it constitutional if the statute involved is a state or local law.

6. Political Questions

Finally there is an interesting class of cases in which the Supreme Court recognizes a valid constitutional issue in a case meeting all the requirements, yet the Supreme Court will not decide the issue. This is the intriguing classification of constitutional issues known as "political questions." If the constitutional question is "political," the Court holds that the constitutional decision is to be made by the political branches of the government. These decisions, made by Congress or the President, are not subject to review in Court.

The questions which are deemed "political" are narrowly restricted. They fall into three general classifications. The first class covers the procedure for amending the Constitution (Article V). The second class concerns the so-called guaranty clause which guarantees to each state a republican form of government (Article IV, Section 4). The third class consists of various aspects of foreign affairs, such as the legality of the "recognition" of a foreign government as the lawful government of that particular foreign country, a question not covered by any specific constitutional provision. Baker v. Carr, 369 U.S. 186 (1962).

The Supreme Court says that these issues are issues which the Constitution relegates by implication to the political branches of the government. So Congress is to decide whether or not the state has a republican form of government by deciding to accept or reject as members of the Congress the duly elected representatives of that state. Concerning foreign affairs, the President is considered to have inherent powers as Head of State in international law. And there is no principle of state powers in our relations with other nations. It follows that there are inherent federal powers to carry on our international relationships. In international matters, the federal government is not bound by the rule concerning internal powers that the federal government can exercise only those powers delegated to it by the Constitution. United States v. Curtiss-Wright Export Corp., 299 U.S. 304 (1936).

The Court has carefully considered whether it should make decisions concerning the process of amending the U. S. Constitution. The case of Coleman v. Miller, 307 U.S. 433 (1939), involved the ratification of a proposed amendment authorizing Congress to ban child labor. The amendment was never ratified; later broader interpretation of the congressional power to regulate commerce established this congressional power. This power was exercised by Congress in enacting the Fair Labor Standards Act of 1938.

In the *Coleman* opinion, the Court detailed a significant and interesting part of American history, the adoption of the Fourteenth Amendment. The Fourteenth Amendment adoption involved serious constitutional issues because three of the governments ratifying it were new governments of southern states erected under Reconstruction after the earlier governments had rejected ratification. Two other states, in the North, had ratified and then passed resolutions purporting to withdraw their ratifications of the amendment. To get the requisite number of states for ratification, the three southern states which had rejected and then under Reconstruction governments had ratified and the two northern states which had ratified and then attempted to reject, all had to be counted as ratifying.

What actually happened was that Congress adopted a resolution requesting the Secretary of State to communicate a list of the states which had ratified. The Secretary included in his list the states which had rejected and later ratified, but he called particular attention to the situation of the two states which had ratified and then had undertaken to withdraw their ratification. On the following day, the Congress simply adopted a concurrent resolution reciting that three-fourths of the states had ratified the Fourteenth Amendment. Necessarily included in this three-fourths were the states which had rejected and then ratified and those that had ratified and attempted to withdraw ratification.

As the Supreme Court said in its opinion in Coleman v. Miller:

> "Thus the political departments of the Government dealt with the effect both of previous rejection and of attempted withdrawal and determined that both were ineffectual in the presence of an actual ratification. * * * This decision by the political departments of the Government as to the va-

lidity of the adoption of the Fourteenth Amendment has been accepted. We think that in accordance with this historic precedent the question of the efficacy of ratifications by state legislatures, in the light of previous rejection or attempted withdrawal, should be regarded as a political question pertaining to the political departments, with the ultimate authority in the Congress in the exercise of its control over the promulgation of the adoption of the amendment." (307 U.S. at 449.)

Political questions constitute only a small percentage of constitutional issues. The normal kinds of constitutional issues with which American citizens are familiar are not political questions and are not likely ever to fall into that category.

The ratification process involving the proposed Equal Rights Amendment (printed at the end of the Constitution in Appendix B) is posing the same constitutional question concerning withdrawal of ratification. Some states have taken such action. The constitutional rule today is the rule of the Fourteenth Amendment ratification that once a state ratifies, it cannot withdraw ratification. But a caveat: this is a constitutional rule established by the Congress under the political questions doctrine. Since Congress makes the final decision on this constitutional issue, it can change its earlier decision, just as the Court can overrule a prior constitutional decision it has made.

7. Conclusion

This chapter has detailed briefly the origins of the doctrine of judicial review and the procedural and policy considerations involved in raising constitutional issues for decision in the United States Supreme Court. We now turn our attention to an analysis of the nature of these constitutional issues. As this analysis is developed, one should constantly be reminded that the Court moves only through flesh-and-blood cases and only in accordance with the jurisdictional and procedural requirements.

CHAPTER 2

THE CONSTITUTIONAL FOUNDATIONS OF LIBERTY

1. The Four Functions of the Constitution

The United States Constitution fulfills four fundamental functions:

1. It establishes a national government: Articles I, II, III, and VI, and Amendments 12, 16, 17, 20, 22, 23, and 25.

2. It controls the relationship between the national government and the governments of the states: Article I, Sections 8 and 10, Article III, Section 2, Article IV, and Amendments 10, 11, 18, and 21.

3. It defines and preserves personal liberty: Article I, Section 9, and Amendments 1–10 (Bill of Rights), 13, 14, 15, 19, 24, and 26.

4. It contains provisions to enable the government to perpetuate itself: Article V.

This quite general analysis can be made more useful by generalizing even further concerning these four functions: The constitutional amending power is a very special power in Article V, essential to the Constitution, but of little direct concern to the substantive provisions of the Constitution which form the heart of what we know as the study of "Constitutional Law."

Further, the first function, setting up a national government, and the second function, relating that national government to the governments of the states, can be treated together as constituting one of the two major aspects of constitutional analysis. This leaves the last of the four functions as the other major aspect of constitutional analysis, the protection of individual liberty. Constitutional personal liberty is the protection of the citizen from governmental power, whether state or federal.

Basic constitutional analysis can, therefore, be divided into two fundamental inquiries. One of these involves the governmental organization and exercise of power. The other involves the protection of the freedoms of the citizens by constitutional provisions.

The teaching materials used to teach Constitutional Law almost invariably consider first the constitutional provisions concerning the establishment of the national government and the relationship between the national government and state governments. Then the materials go on to consider the protections of individual liberty.

This analysis is historically acceptable. It is not, however, analytically sound. The earlier important cases in constitutional law had to do with the organization and powers of the national government and how the exercise of those powers related to the powers of the state governments because we left the protection of liberty largely to the states. It is only in comparative recent constitutional history that we have begun to have what is now an exciting and almost overwhelming flood of decisions concerning individual liberty. So the historical approach reaches liberty last.

It is not analytically sound to consider the organization of the federal government and its relationship to the state governments before considering the constitutional aspects of individual liberty because constitutional questions concerning the protection of individual liberty arise in all constitutional cases, including those allocating governmental power to the national government or the state governments. So any analysis of the cases involving the distribution of powers between the states and federal government postpones the fundamental inquiry contained in all such cases as to whether either government has the power to engage in the regulatory activity involved, or whether, on the other hand, neither the state governments nor the national government can regulate because such regulation would interfere with individual liberty. Examples showing this liberty/governmental power relationship will be given after further foundation is laid.

2. Liberty Against Government: The Basic Analysis

To aid in understanding the nature of the distinction between liberty and the exercise of governmental power and to give us the foundation for the constitutional analysis, let us develop a simple imaginary concept which will be used throughout this book.

Imagine, if you will, that we took all of the power that any government could have and placed it in a huge oblong box. Included in this box would be the most autocractic and despotic powers of government. Along with other generally acceptable governmental powers in our box, then, would be the power to execute someone without trial or without charges. So also would be included the power to throw a person in jail for criticizing the government, or the power to take a person's home and his or her other property without any excuse and without compensating for it. Other despotic powers would include forcing all citizens to wear a uniform, to attend a state church, to listen to a governmental leader's speech. So assume, if you will, in the box are all possible governmental powers, including the most despicable and the ugliest exercises of power, such as occurred in Nazi Germany.

In the United States under our Constitution, we saw this long oblong box into two parts. We shall represent this by drawing a vertical line through the box as shown:

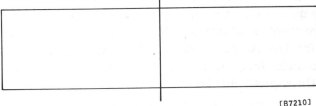

[B7210]

The reason for cutting the box apart is to take away from the government those powers which we do not want our government to have. We take away the powers of the despot. We protect the individual citizen against intrusions upon freedom of speech and freedom of religion. We require fair court procedures. We insist that the citizen can be fined or imprisoned only on fair charges involving a valid offense and after a fair and complete trial. So we set aside a large part of this box of potential governmental powers. We insist that our government cannot have the powers which would infringe upon our liberty.

After we have severed these excessive and undesirable governmental powers out of our total aggregation of powers, we set them aside. We call governmental attempts to control in these protected areas invasions of "freedom" or "individual liberty" or, as we shall see later, we often just call them the protections of "due process of law" as a shorthand expression. We accomplish this withdrawal of possible governmental powers by writing into the Constitution a Bill of Rights and other protections of individual liberty.

So now our box of governmental power looks like this:

On the left side, within the dotted lines, we have that part of the original box of governmental powers where power has been taken away from our government under our system. We call that area: liberty. On the right side are the remaining governmental powers. Those are the powers which are not taken away by our constitutional requirement for liberty. It is the Constitution which has severed our box by drawing the line which protects our liberties from governmental powers.

A word of caution here; although our schematic line is drawn down the middle of our diagram, it was carefully said that the box was sawed into two parts, not sawed in half. There is no attempt by the placement of the line to show how much governmental power has been taken out of the total potential amount. At the moment, we are not interested in the quantity of governmental power. We are interested in the nature of the qualities of the powers involved.

To understand the application of this boxlike configuration, which will more often now be called a diagram, consider a simple, although very important, constitutional issue. A person makes a speech advocating revoluntionary overthrow of the government. As most readers probably already know, this revolutionary advocacy is not automatically subject to criminal penalties by the government. If this advocacy of revolution is advocacy in the abstract, philosophical sense, we have adequate constitutional holdings establishing that it is protected free speech. Only when the advocacy becomes advocacy for immediate, significant revolutionary or antigovernmental action may the speaker be punished for such statements.

[*39*]

In terms of our diagram, the issue in such a case is simply whether this case falls on the left side of the dividing line, in the area of individual freedom (the government may not prohibit the speech)①, or falls on the right side in the area of governmental power (the government does have the power to control the speech) ②:

Liberty	Governmental Power
①	②

[B7212]

To make this analysis clearer, consider some other examples. A book is charged with being obscene. Is it protected free speech, or is it a book which is not protected free speech and, therefore, can be prohibited from circulation by the government? The issue in terms of our diagram is whether the result of the case falls in the area of individual liberty on the left side—①, or in the area of governmental power on the right —②. The vertical line which cuts apart our box-diagram is the dividing line between personal liberty on one side and governmental power to control the activities and conduct of persons on the other.

[40]

Virtually all constitutional issues involving individual liberty are subject to this simple representation, although the decision in many cases is a difficult and intricate one and is not predicted by the diagram. The purpose of this simplified analysis is not to indicate that constitutional decision-making is easy. It is for the purpose of showing the nature of constitutional issues.

Implicit in the description of the nature of individual liberty set out above is a fundamental consideration. Constitutional individual liberty in our system of government, with some limited exceptions described later, is almost always an issue of individual freedom against *governmental power*. It consists of the protection of the individual from overreaching or undue intrusion *by the government*. Liberty, in constitutional definition, usually does not consist of individual freedom from intrusions by other private citizens. We protect freedom from intrusion by other private citizens with laws making certain conduct crimes. These laws against theft of property, intrusions upon privacy, and the like, are not constitutional protections.

This point is fundamental. It can be demonstrated with an example. Able, a private citizen, accosts another private citizen, Baker, and robs him of his billfold containing $100 and other property. Has the Constitution been violated?

Clearly not. Yet consider: certainly citizen Baker has been, in the words of the Constitution, "deprived of his property without due process of law." But it is not unconstitutional for private citizen Able to rob private citizen Baker because the Constitution prohibits only the *government,* state or federal, from depriving a citizen of property without due process of law. The protection of the individual citizen's right not to have his money taken from him by another private citizen is contained in the criminal law enacted by the state government. It is a protection created by the government, not a protection contained in the Constitution. Only if the government takes the property of a citizen without paying him for it is the Constitution violated.

This principle, which is absolutely basic to the understanding of constitutional rights, explains why it is important to emphasize that it is the limitations upon *governmental* power which are represented on the left side of the diagram. It bears repeating: constitutional liberty in our system is usually the protection of the individual from governmental intrusion, not protection of the individual from illegal aggressive actions by other private citizens.

This very fundamental principle is subject to narrow exceptions. The three major ones are found (1) in the Thirteenth Amendment, (2) in the federal government's power to control federal elections, and (3) in situations involving a loosely defined "right to travel" or right to move from place to place.

Look carefully at the wording of the Thirteenth Amendment. The wording is peculiar when compared to the wording of the Bill of Rights and the critical Fourteenth Amendment. The Bill of Rights (the first eight amendments) and the Fourteenth Amendment refer to official actions of the state or federal governments. For example, the First Amendment prohibits laws of Congress interfering with the free exercise of religion or freedom of speech. Criminal trials, which are the subject of much of our specific constitutional protections in the Bill of Rights, obviously are federal or state governmental activity. The language of the Fourteenth Amendment prohibits a "state" from depriving any person of life, liberty, or property without due process of law.

But, the Thirteenth Amendment, prohibiting slavery, does not contain words limited to action by government. A private citizen can violate the Thirteenth Amendment. There have been cases where private citizens have been found guilty of violating the Thirteenth Amendment by holding someone in involuntary servitude, or in a state of peonage. These are rare cases, but they can occur.

Further, in recent years, the Court has interpreted the Thirteenth Amendment to constitute a fairly broad prohibition against private citizens discriminating against other private citizens on a racial basis. The theory is that racial discrimination constitutes a "badge of slavery." Details of this recent important development are set out in Chapter 4 on Congressional Protection of Constitutional Liberties.

The second example of private-citizen violation of the Constitution involves cases where it has been held that one person's interference with another's right to vote in a national election is in violation of the Constitution itself, not simply a violation of a criminal statute. This follows from recognition by the Court that constitutional provision for federal elections implies constitutional protection of their sanctity even from private citizen interference.

The third example of a constitutional liberty not defined restrictively as protecting the person against only the government's actions is the recently recognized "right to travel" or right to move from place to place. This is the undergirding constitutional principle which has resulted in recent holdings which have severely limited the length of residence requirements of the states for purposes of voting, attending local public schools, or being entitled to placement on local welfare rolls. These are found to be situations involving the possible denial by governmental action of a right to travel. But this right has also been recognized by the Court as giving Congress the power to pass legislation to punish private citizens who interfere with the right of other citizens to go from one place to another to engage in political activity. Private citizens in the south who obstructed blacks in their use of public highways and other public facilities were found to violate the constitutional rights of the black private citizens. U. S. v. Guest, 383 U.S. 745 (1966). It is in this latter kind of situation that the right is not merely defined against governmental intrusion but also is defined against private citizen infringement.

Compared to the great bulk of Supreme Court decisions which define and protect liberty, these instances are exceptional. It is important to understand that in most of the cases involving individual liberty, we are talking in terms of the freedom of the citizen from control by the federal or state governments.

It can be difficult to decide what constitutes governmental control or action in particular situations. It might be that a government interferes with someone's liberty by not taking protective action on the citizen's behalf. The action of the government may be indirect or passive in the sense that the government is simply contributing in part to the actions of what otherwise seems to be a private group or a private body. Failure of a sheriff to try to prevent a lynching is a stark example of this "passive" governmental action.

In summary, it should be understood that for present purposes and subject only to the unusual exceptions mentioned above, when we refer to individual liberty, constitutional freedoms, or due process of law, we are referring to protecting the individual from action of the government which might infringe upon those freedoms. In the terms of the diagram we are developing, the issue is between liberty on the one side and governmental power on the other.

3. Liberty and the Federal System: Basic Analysis

These questions of individual liberty are the first of the two major and fundamental classifications of constitutional issues outlined earlier in this chapter. The other classification can best be demonstrated by returning to our diagram. Only after it has been decided that the constitutional question does not fall in the area of freedom—of individual liberty—does this second constitutional question arise. It does not arise at all in most nations; it does not arise in Great Britain, for example. But it does arise in the United States, because ours is a federal system. Under our Constitution, we take the governmental powers remaining after the denial of power which constitutes liberty and divide them into two units— state and federal. This is how it appears in simplified form on our diagram:

Liberty	Governmental Power
	Federal
	State

[B7218]

Again, there must be a word of caution. In our division there is no attempt to indicate the quantitative distribution of power between the state and federal governments. This new line is only a stylized representation of the fact that in a federal system we divide our governmental power into federal power and state power. Further, this aspect of our diagram is highly unrefined. Later, we reach questions of the distribution of power between state and federal governments. We shall then refine the diagram to illustrate the more intricate nature of the allocation of federal and state power.

But the second of the two fundamental classifications of constitutional questions in the United States is the issue involving our federal system: Which government has the power to engage in this kind of regulation. Or, perhaps, can both governments do so? Note this issue need be considered only after it has been decided that government may take action—only after it is decided that this particular governmental action does not fall in the prohibited area of individual freedom.

Sometimes it is helpful to posit a hypothetical situation which is extreme and even somewhat ridiculous, because it can be used effectively to explain the nature of the analysis. Let us assume such a situation to see how constitutional issues may arise with respect to both fundamental constitutional questions: (1) individual liberty; (2) distribution of power between state and federal governments. Suppose that a *state* passed a law requiring all United States coins containing copper and silver to be turned in to the state government with compensation in new aluminum or steel U. S. coins of the same denomination. The motive of the state's action would be obvious. The state could recover the silver and copper from the coins, sell the precious metals, and add money to its treasury. Thereby, maybe, a possible need for an increase on its sales tax could be avoided!

A citizen wishes to protest the enforcement of this law, claiming that it interferes with his or her individual liberty. He asserts the state may not take the silver and copper coins which are part of his coin collection, held in great affection, and compel that the coins be given up in exchange for shiny new coins of the same denomination but made of aluminum or steel and intrinsically not as valuable. The coin collector asserts that he is being deprived of property without due process of law.

But with good legal advice, the citizen will also assert an additional contention. The coin collector will assert that even though it is decided that the government may force citizens to give up their coin collections and take in return other coins of the same face value, the *state* government has no power to do this—that under our constitutional system only the *federal* government can do it. The assertion will be that the federal government's power over its coins and currency is an exclusive power and is forbidden to the states.

Our citizen has two chances to win the case. He may win on the individual liberty claim which is that neither government, state nor federal, can force him to give up his silver and copper coins for ones of the same face value but of less intrinsic value. But even losing on that point, he may be successful in his claim that state governments in our system have no power to deal with U. S. money; that only the federal government has the power to do so.

Our result in this case is no mystery. On the basis of cases which arose as the result of the United States government going off the gold standard and requiring citizens to turn in gold coins in the middle 1930's, we can be more certain in this case than we can in most constitutional cases how this case will come out. The Supreme Court should be expected to hold that the citizen may be compelled, as against the claim of individual liberty, to turn in the "coin of the realm" and be compensated only for the face value through new coins of the same denomination.

But our citizen in this hypothetical case will, nevertheless, win the case. The constitutional decisions clearly indicate that the coinage of money and the establishment of money as legal tender is a matter exclusively for the federal government and that the states have no control or power over our monetary system.

The first issue in our case was whether the result fell on the side of individual liberty or on the side of governmental power. The decision is on the side of governmental power. But then by showing affirmatively that the governmental power to engage in this activity is lodged wholly

in the federal government, our citizen wins. Let
us place this case on our simple box-diagram:

Liberty	Governmental Power
(Citizen's liberty claim fails ⊗)	③ Federal
	(⊗ State's power claim fails) State

[B7194]

The result in this case is found in the federal portion of the governmental power representation—
③. The citizen fails in the claim of liberty—①.
But the citizen wins because, by showing the
power to regulate is solely in federal hands—③,
the state's assertion of power to regulate fails—
②. Only if the Court had found that power lay
in the state, could the state win this case.

From the consideration of this simple situation,
we now know a case nearly always involves both
basic constitutional issues. But the second issue
of distribution of power between state and federal
governments is pertinent only if the decision is in
favor of governmental power as against individual freedom. These two questions follow in logical
sequence. This is why we turn our attention

[51]

first to defining constitutional liberty—freedom of the individual from control by the government.

4. Responsibility for Protecting Liberty

Before we enter into an analysis of the substantive approach to these freedom questions by the Supreme Court, one other basic matter must be mentioned and then postponed for later consideration. It involves a concept that can be difficult to understand, yet it is important that it be understood.

In the usual constitutional case, what is happening is that the Supreme Court itself is defining and enforcing the individual liberty against the governmental action. What we actually have is one branch of the government, the Court, protecting the citizen from another branch of the government, legislative or executive.

In sharp contrast, we hear less of the fact that the Congress and the Executive also may act to protect and define individual liberty against governmental action. Note that the last sections of the Thirteenth, Fourteenth, and Fifteenth Amendments, and the last paragraph of the Nineteenth Amendment authorize *the Congress* to enforce the amendments by appropriate legislation. If and when Congress does this, its actions mean that the Congress itself is enforcing individual liberty. Thus, congressional enforcement of constitutional liberty is not as unusual as it seems. The Congress has passed various civil rights acts. Many of these are passed as a means of protecting individual constitutional liberties against governmental action. What Congress is doing in these instances is creating enforcement mechanisms such as criminal penalties or civil liability against public officers who deprive someone of constitutional rights. Congress is not defining those rights.

In the analysis of our diagram, many of these civil rights acts are an exercise of federal legislative power, just like federal judicial power, enforcing the liberty side of our diagram by opposing governmental power exercised by some public official. On analysis, the critical point is that congressional actions to enforce individual liberty are similar to Supreme Court decisions protecting individual liberty. In this instance, the government is acting on the liberty side of our diagram *through the Congress* just as it much more usually acts on the liberty side of the diagram through the courts.

To summarize this principle, let us visualize again the left side of our diagram, the side where we have cut off governmental power which infringes upon the activity of persons. We can insert under that left side of the diagram the following brief description of how those individual liberties are enforced:

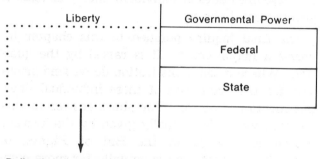

Liberty	Governmental Power
	Federal
	State

Defined and enforced in most instances by Court decision, but also enforced (but not defined) by the passage of "civil rights" legislation in Congress and by the President's actions carrying out court decisions and enforcing civil rights legislation.

[B7195]

5. The Constitutional Sources of Liberty

Most of the excitement engendered by constitutional decisions of the last generation has been the result of their defining individual liberty. Free speech decisions, freedom of religion decisions, the decisions compelling racial integration in the public schools and eliminating racial discrimination throughout society, the one-person, one-vote decisions, the abortion decision, the great mass of decisions setting out in detail the requirements for a fair trial in criminal cases— all these are issues of individual liberty as against governmental power.

The final inquiry pursued in this chapter involves a major point. It is raised by the question: Where in the Constitution do we find provision for the protection of these individual liberties mentioned above. The short answer to this question which is normally given by the average citizen is: "Why, in the Bill of Rights, of course!" The problem is actually far more complicated. The first ten amendments to the Constitution are commonly referred to as the Bill of Rights. They were passed all at one time, and virtually contemporaneously with the adoption of the Constitution. On a slightly more sophisticated level, the Bill of Rights is viewed as including only the first eight amendments, since the Ninth and Tenth are general catch-all provisions. It is almost certain that the states would not have adopted the Constitution if those amendments, written by James Madison, had not been promised for immediate inclusion.

An understanding of the scope of the first ten amendments is dependent upon an understanding of the historical situation surrounding the adoption of the Constitution. Recall that the Articles of Confederation had failed. We had attempted to create a nation out of a group of independent states, and our attempt was a failure. The union was floundering because the central government which was designed to hold the states together in one nation was too weak to carry out this task.

With prescient wisdom the founders saw that for our nation to endure there must be more strength in the central government. Yet our nation had just gone through the blood bath of the Revolutionary War to break away from a strong unified government, and we genuinely feared the creation of a national government which was too powerful. The states were the established governments. They had their own strong constitutions with their own bills of rights.

The purpose of the adoption of the Bill of Rights in the United States Constitution, therefore, was to protect individual citizens against the federal government—the federal government only. It was clear to the states at the time of their adoption of the Constitution that the first ten amendments were meant to apply only to the federal government. While only the First Amendment was quite specific and precise on this point, the understanding covered all the amendments. This understanding was confirmed relatively early in our constitutional history by a Supreme Court decision. Barron v. The Mayor and

City Council of Baltimore, 32 U.S. (7 Pet.) 243 (1833).

The implications of this early principle and early decision were far-reaching. There was no protection of a citizen's right of free speech in the United States Constitution if it was a state law which restricted the speech. Nor was there a protection of the freedom of religion or of the various procedural criminal guarantees from intrusion by state law or by state criminal process. The citizen under the United States Constitution could claim the protections of the Bill of Rights only when it was the federal government taking actions prohibited by those core provisions. It was assumed that the strong state governments and strong state courts bound by their bills of rights would protect citizens from intrusion upon personal liberties by the states.

The Civil War brought about a complete constitutional reorientation with respect to individual freedom. Until the Civil War those who were concerned about personal liberty feared a strong federal government and did not fear the state governments. The Civil War was a demonstration to the American people that the states could not be trusted to preserve liberty, that the states were willing to secede from the Union and mount an attempted revolution to avoid giving to human beings the basic human liberty of freedom from bondage.

The Thirteenth, Fourteenth, and Fifteenth Amendments were a direct outgrowth of the Civil War. The Thirteenth Amendment, relatively narrow in scope, abolished slavery. The Fifteenth Amendment undertook to preserve the right to vote regardless of race, color, or previous condition of servitude. But the Fourteenth Amendment was the great constitutional pronouncement which was to bring about a revolution in constitutional liberty.

There is an unresolved historical debate about the scope of the Fourteenth Amendment. Was the first section designed to make all the protections of the Bill of Rights applicable to the states? If so, the federal government and the federal courts would become responsible for insuring that the states did not interfere with free speech, freedom of religion, procedural protections, and the other rights listed in the first eight amendments.

A strong argument can be made for the proposition that the amendment was designed to do this. The particular words most apt to do so are contained at the beginning of the second sentence of the first section: "No State shall make or enforce any law which shall abridge the privileges and immunities of citizens of the United States; * * *." What were these privileges and immunities? Most likely, they were to be the constitutional protections of personal freedom found in the Bill of Rights and wherever else they may appear in the Constitution. If these are not the privileges and immunities of United States citizens, it is hard to conceive of what would be.

On the other side of the argument, it can be said that if the framers of the amendment were being precise about "reading the Bill of Rights into the Fourteenth Amendment," more effective and clearer words would have been chosen. An answer to this argument, is, of course, that in drafting words for a constitutional provision, the framers do not want to speak in precise and restrictive terms because they want to leave some latitude for later development and interpretation. Additionally, there was a further practical political matter. It would likely have been impossible to get the Fourteenth Amendment adopted if it had spelled out too precisely a full incorporation of the Bill of Rights.

This historical dispute has permeated decisions of the Supreme Court right up to the present time. There is now a split among the current Court membership in the most recent decisions as to whether the framers actually intended that the protections of the Bill of Rights be made applicable to the states through the Fourteenth Amendment. The late Justice Black took the firm position that they were made applicable; and the late

Justice Harlan held the firm position that they were not, that the Fourteenth Amendment "stands * * * on its own bottom." Griswold v. Connecticut, 381 U.S. 479, 500 (1965). While Justice Black's view has largely prevailed, Justice Powell on the current Court still insists, as did Justice Harlan, that the scope of the rights set out in the first eight amendments is different when applied to the states. It is his view that the states have more leeway in controlling criminal procedures and applying other provisions of the Bill of Rights. Apodaca v. Oregon, 406 U.S. 404 (1972) (concurring opinion).

The development in the Court of its view concerning the role of the Fourteenth Amendment in making state intrusions against individual liberty subject to control under the U. S. Constitution is an instructive history in how constitutional law grows and changes.

The key decision came early, only five years after the adoption of the Fourteenth Amendment. In 1873 in the Slaughter-House Cases, 83 U.S. (16 Wall.) 36, the Court turned firmly away from finding that in the "privileges or immunities" clause of the amendment, the Bill of Rights had been made applicable to the states. The plaintiff challenged a state-created business monopoly in slaughterhouses asserting that his right to engage in the slaughterhouse business, prohibited by the government-created monopoly, was a "privilege or immunity" of a United States citizen under the Fourteenth Amendment. The Court denied his right to engage in the slaughterhouse business. The impact of the decision was that the citizen was not entitled to claim liberties against state intrusion in the United States Constitution; he could look only to the constitution of his state.

This decision and others which followed completely gutted the so-called "privilege or immunities" clause of the Fourteenth Amendment. Only one case has ever held that this constitutional provision was violated, Colgate v. Harvey, 296 U. S. 404 (1935), and that case was overruled five years later. Madden v. Kentucky, 309 U.S. 83 (1940). So the lofty sounding words came to mean nothing.

Pressures grew on the Court, however, to protect citizens against the regulatory activities of the states. The states could infringe free speech, could take private property without paying just compensation, could fail to give the protections of fair criminal procedures. Cases began to flow to the Supreme Court in the late years of the nineteenth century in which citizens had been seriously abused by their own states and had not found protection in their state constitutions or in their own state courts. The United States Supreme Court indicated reluctance to assume this tremendous control over the states, but under the pressure of the cases and in this vacuum of power to protect liberties, it acquiesced.

After the Slaughter-House Cases and other similar cases which followed, and before the Supreme Court began to move into the area of protecting individual liberty as against state governments, our basic diagram of constitutional power looked like this:

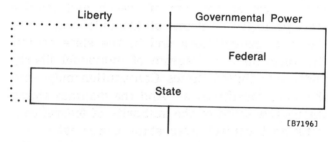

Now we are for the first time engaging in a quantitative evaluation as we examine this diagram. As far as the United States Constitution was concerned, there was very little protection of liberty against state intrusion. The protection against the federal government, of course, was broad because of the Bill of Rights. We draw our line indicating the sweep of state power as against the liberty claim still leaving some protection of liberty against the states, but not very much. Under Article I, Sections 9 and 10, of the

Constitution, we find a few limitations upon state power. Some of these protect individual liberty, such as the prohibitions against the passage of *ex post facto* laws, against the suspension of the privilege of the writ of habeas corpus, and against states passing laws interfering with the obligation of contracts. But this was all.

The federal government engaged in very little general regulation at that time so the important rights such as freedom of speech and religion were protected in almost all instances only under the state constitutions and in the state courts. Our diagram is a diagram of individual liberty under our United States Constitution only—not the state constitutions. And the diagram shows the narrow scope of the authority of federal constitutional control over state power when the states were charged with intruding upon the rights of citizens.

At the end of the last century, the Supreme Court began a gradual process of taking provisions from the Bill of Rights (applicable only to the federal government) and making them applicable to the states by "reading them into" the Fourteenth Amendment. The great wording of the "privileges and immunities" clause had been destroyed as an effective constitutional provision by the Court. So the Court used another clause which seemed to be narrower in its wording—"due process of law."

The phrase "due process of law" could well have been taken as applying only to fair criminal procedures. But under the words of the Fourteenth Amendment which prohibit any state from depriving "any person of life, liberty, or property without due process of law; * * * ," the Supreme Court began the gradual process of "reading into" the Fourteenth Amendment the protections of the Bill of Rights and making them applicable to the states. The case instituting this process is the 1897 case, Chicago, Burlington, and Quincy R. R. Co. v. Chicago, 166 U.S. 226. It was there held to be a denial of "due process of law" under the Fourteenth Amendment when a state deprived a citizen of property without just compensation within the meaning of the so-called "eminent domain" provisions of the Fifth Amendment. Eminent domain is the governmental power to condemn private property for public use—take title to it—by paying just compensation.

It is startling to us today to realize, in the sweep of American constitutional history, it was not until 1925 in the case of Gitlow v. New York, 268 U.S. 652, that the Court for the first time "read into" the Fourteenth Amendment and made applicable to the states the First Amendment protection of freedom of speech. So it was not until

135 years after the adoption of the Constitution that the Supreme Court recognized and established its power to protect an individual citizen in his free speech liberty against an oppressive state law. And, it was not until 1940, in the case of Cantwell v. Connecticut, 310 U.S. 296, that the First Amendment freedom of religion was made applicable to the states by reading it into the "due process of law" clause of the Fourteenth Amendment.

These cases show that since 1897 the history of constitutional development of liberty against exercises of state regulatory power has been a history of the gradual inclusion of the protections of the Bill of Rights in the Fourteenth Amendment through the use of the "due process of law" clause. In our diagram the effect of these decisions has been to shrink the area of state intrusion into the field of individual liberty in accordance with the dotted lines and the arrow:

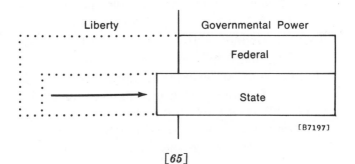

The history of the more recent years has been a very rapid carrying over into the "due process" clause of the Fourteenth Amendment the criminal procedural protections of the Fourth, Fifth, Sixth, and Eighth Amendments. These include the privilege against self-incrimination, protection against unreasonable search and seizure, right to counsel, jury trials in criminal cases, protection against double jeopardy (against being tried over and over again for the same offense), and others as well.

As of our time all of the Bill of Rights has been made applicable to the states through the reading of its provisions into the "due process of law" clause of the Fourteenth Amendment except for the Fifth Amendment requirement of indictment by grand jury and the Seventh Amendment right to jury trials in civil as opposed to criminal cases. As a practical matter, every other provision of the first eight amendments to the Constitution is now equally as applicable to the states under the Fourteenth Amendment as it is applicable to the federal government by virtue of being contained specifically in the Bill of Rights.

In the last few years the Supreme Court has become so familiar with accepting the application of the Bill of Rights to the states through the "due process of law" clause of the Fourteenth Amendment that often the Court no longer even refers to the Fourteenth Amendment. Instead in a free speech case, the Court may simply indicate that it is testing the state limitation on speech as against the "First Amendment" claim.

The history is important to know, however, because the earlier cases refer to a concept of "selectively incorporating" only portions of the Bill of Rights into the Fourteenth Amendment. Knowing that there was a gradual process of incorporation is the only way that these earlier cases can be explained and understood.

In spite of the extent to which the Court has now expanded those simple words, "due process of law," of the Fourteenth Amendment to cover virtually all of the Bill of Rights, it is probable that the two remaining requirements will not soon be made applicable to the states. The states' tradition of charging criminal offenses by information (by the prosecutor simply filing a charge) rather than by grand jury indictment is so well established that it would be rather an unexpected intrusion for the Court suddenly to hold that all charges had to be by grand jury indictment. The constitutional provision as it applies to the federal government is considered to be somewhat of an anachronism, so extension to the states would not be likely.

This is even more true of the requirement of jury trials in civil cases. The overall trend is very strongly away from requiring jury trial in civil, as opposed to criminal, cases. In Great Britain the use of a jury in a civil case is virtually unknown today except in cases involving defamation. Many of the states of the United States restrict the use of the jury in private lawsuits between citizens. It is more likely that at this time the development of the constitutional "reading in" process is now complete.

The reverse of the "reading in" process described above has also taken place in the interpretation and application of the Constitution. The constitutional provision today which is most commonly the source of cases involving the "liberty against government" inquiry is the provision of the Fourteenth Amendment prohibiting the states from passing any laws denying "the equal protection of the laws." This is the constitutional provision upon which virtually all of the sweeping cases eliminating racial, religious, sex, and national origin discriminations are based. We owe the modern law eliminating racial segregation in public schools and in all other public facilities to the "equal protection" clause. The modern cases involving the fair treatment of students and faculty in schools, of prisoners, of persons on welfare, and in many other aspects of our life are based usually upon equal protection "classification" issues. The equal protection concept demands that citizens be treated fairly when compared to each other. It does not require a fundamental constitutional right to be applicable. Thus, a state is not required by the Constitution to furnish free public education. But if it does have free public schools, then it must make them available without racial, sex, religious, wealth, and other discriminations. San Antonio Independent School Dist. v. Rodriguez, 411 U.S. 1 (1973).

The Supreme Court has recently referred to racial and some other classifications in the law as "suspect" classifications and discrimination according to such classifications are "invidious." The Court finds those classifications unconstitutional unless there is an overwhelmingly strong justification for the government to uphold them. Loving v. Virginia, 388 U.S. 1 (1967).

The Court has refused to find sex discrimination a "suspect" classification, because it continues to find justifications for some discriminations based upon sex. Nevertheless, the Court's record of the last few years in eliminating unreasonable and unjustifiable sex discriminations is a good one. The net effect of the proposed Equal Rights Amendment would be to change sex discrimination to a "suspect" classification under the equal protection of the laws clause. This suspect classification would mean that it would be harder for the Court to uphold a discrimination based upon sex than it now is. It would, for example, be difficult to uphold the current law which provides for the potential drafting of males into the armed forces but not females. It would be more difficult to uphold as constitutional public schools or universities which separate the sexes but are clearly equal in quality. It would be more difficult or impossible to uphold a few distinctions which now exist, some favorable to women and some unfavorable such as authorizing special tax exemptions for widows and not widowers but authorizing the disqualification of pregnant women from disability insurance programs. As an aside, however, it is generally agreed it would not require unisex rest-rooms and locker rooms because compulsory unisex in such situations is not fundamental to constitutional liberty.

Equal protection of the laws is the one arena in which a constitutional provision playing a major role in preserving individual liberty is by its terms applicable only to the states and not to the federal government. The prohibition against states denying the equal protection of the laws follows immediately the "due process of law" clause in the Fourteenth Amendment. But look back at the Fifth Amendment, where the "due process of law" clause applicable to the federal government is found, and look everywhere else in the Bill of Rights. You will find no similar "equal protection of the laws" provision applicable to the federal government.

Court decisions today, however, hold that the principle of equal protection of the laws is now applicable to the federal government's control of individual citizen rights. Here is an instance where a provision of the Constitution referring only to the states had to be "read into" the Bill of Rights to make it applicable to the federal government. This is exactly the reverse process of reading the Bill of Rights into the Fourteenth Amendment. In terms of our diagram, the process has been:

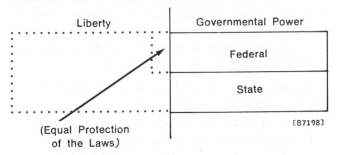

(Equal Protection of the Laws)

The modern development of shrinking the federal power to engage in such classifications can be said to stem largely from the school integration decisions. When the Supreme Court decided the great case leading to the elimination of racially segregated public schools, Brown v. Board of Education of Topeka (Kansas), 347 U.S. 483,

349 U.S. 294 (1954, 1955), the Court also had before it a case challenging racial segregation in the public schools of the District of Columbia. So the Court was faced specifically and precisely with the problem of deciding whether there was a comparable constitutional liberty for pupils to attend a nonracially segregated school under federal jurisdiction in the District of Columbia. On the same day the Court handed down its first *Brown* decision, the Court decided Bolling v. Sharpe, 347 U.S. 497 (1954), unanimously holding that in spite of the lack of an "equal protection of the laws" clause in the Bill of Rights, such discrimination is a violation of "due process of law."

For a period of time following that case, the Court maintained the principle that the federal government might have somewhat greater freedom to discriminate in classifications than would the states because of the lack of an equal protection of the laws clause in the Fifth Amendment or elsewhere in the Bill of Rights. It is more accurate to say today, however, the Court will protect just as broadly and completely against unfair and unreasonable classifications created by federal law as it does against improper classifications created by state law.

With the most minor exceptions, we can then say today that the scope of individual liberty in

our Constitution is of the same breadth whether
the alleged intrusion upon the liberty arises from
the federal government or from a state government.   The minor exceptions to this, e. g., the
two parts of the Bill of Rights not "read into"
the Fourteenth Amendment, do not approach any
issue that we today view as fundamental to liberty.   The scope of free speech, freedom of religion,
fair criminal procedures is exactly the same today whether the federal government or a state is
creating the possible intrusion upon the liberty.
While the courts have not yet been clear and precise on the matter, we can be confident that the
scope of the constitutional protection against discriminations is the same whether the threat of
the unconstitutional discrimination arises from
the federal government or from a state.

6. Conclusion

We began this chapter with a box in which all
possible government power had been placed.   We
have cut apart the box and separated off a great
bulk of potential governmental power which cannot be exercised under our system, because to do
so would intrude upon constitutionally defined
personal liberties.

We turn our attention now to a brief analytical
study of how actual constitutional cases in important areas of liberty fit into our box-diagram

[*73*]

analysis. We shall find that at least in some instances, analysis by some courts has been faulty, because it failed to realize that constitutional liberty stands in opposition to governmental power. We cannot usefully consider the exercise of governmental power until we first consider the possibility that the exercise of official power intrudes into the sacred area of liberty.

CHAPTER 3

THE ROLE OF THE COURTS IN DEFINING AND PROTECTING LIBERTY

1. Substantive and Procedural Due Process of Law

The preceding chapter establishes the fundamental analysis of constitutional liberty. This chapter will apply that analysis to specific cases and situations.

The basic pattern of the distinction between liberty and governmental power is present in virtually all constitutional cases. In many of them, we are not seriously concerned about liberty issues because we are certain that the governmental power does exist to engage in the particular regulation. A 55 mile an hour speed limit for automobiles, a law that requires dangerous drugs to be issued only under prescription, a law setting a minimum wage for employees, a law providing for the licensing and rigid control of the banking business, a law licensing television stations are all examples of general governmental regulation in which we do not perceive serious issues of individual liberty. In our diagram, all of these cases fall on the right-hand side of the dividing line between liberty and governmental power. And there are, of course, a multitude of other routine governmental laws which fall in the same category.

These laws do not raise liberty issues, however, only because they fall in a range of acceptability. A 55 mile an hour speed limit is reasonable and acceptable. What about a nationwide ten mile an hour speed limit? Or a one mile an hour speed limit? Think of all the lives that would be saved if nobody could travel more than one mile an hour. But is such a rigid restriction not an invasion of liberty? The question in this situation is a real one.

How dangerous must a dangerous drug be before it can be limited to prescription or banned entirely? This is also a question of liberty. Possibly a minimum wage can be set so high that individual rights are infringed. We license television stations today. But suppose that we outlawed television. A deeply troublesome question of liberty involving free speech, freedom of expression, is implicit in control of television which is too extreme or too rigid.

The reality is, however, that in our democratic society these extremes normally do not occur as part of our usual governmental regulation, so liberty questions are not serious. But liberty questions lurk in all such cases. There will be additional discussion concerning the liberty issues in general governmental regulation in Chapter 5. But the usual analysis with respect to such regulation is that most laws fall in our diagram on the side of authorized governmental power and not on the side of liberty.

Drawing the critical dividing line between liberty and governmental power in those particular cases where the liberty issue does seriously arise is the most basic of all constitutional issues. We turn our attention then to those cases in which there is a serious liberty question—where liberty must be constitutionally defined. We first look at the basic nature of a liberty case. Then we shall follow a step-by-step evaluation to show some instances where this analysis aids in the resolution of constitutional issues. We shall also see some instances of mistakes in constitutional approach revealed by this analysis.

One word of limitation is necessary. This book is not a textbook on constitutional law. It does not attempt to state and critique the substantive constitutional principles of all fields of the law. The discussion of particular cases is meant to reveal that the analysis is functional in explaining what the court is doing. But some cases will show also how the Court sometimes goes wrong in its analysis.

We start with some "controversial" recent and fairly recent cases of the Supreme Court. They can show the analysis in operation to reveal what the Court is actually doing as it relates liberty to governmental power.

Certainly the most controversial constitutional decision of the last few years is Roe v. Wade, 410 U.S. 113 (1973). This is the case which held that during the first trimester of pregnancy the pregnant woman has the freedom to choose to have an abortion so long as she can find a physician who is willing to administer one. In constitutional analysis, this means that the right to choose to have an abortion under these circumstances is a liberty protected by that clause of the Fourteenth Amendment and of the Fifth Amendment which prohibits governmental intrusion upon life, liberty, or property without due process of law. The government cannot by law prohibit such abortions.

A dispute about whether Roe v. Wade was correctly or incorrectly decided still rages today. But our concern here is with the nature of the decision as a matter of constitutional analysis.

Before the case was decided, the practical conclusion has to have been that the regulation of abortion by government was a constitutionally accepted governmental power. Abortion has been a criminal offense both for the pregnant woman and the doctor since the beginning of our nation. And now, suddenly, because of a decision by the United States Supreme Court, abortion becomes a constitutional right of the pregnant woman and a constitutional right for a doctor to perform an abortion.

In terms of our analysis, this means that the line dividing liberty and governmental power has been moved to encompass this case in the area of liberty. Governmental power has been shrunk by a constitutional decision of the Supreme Court which enlarges the area of liberty. By analysis, this enlargement is and must be at the expense of the sweep of governmental power authorized under the Constitution. In the diagram, we represent the case of Roe v. Wade, or the right to an abortion, with asterisks—one asterisk under state power and one under federal power. While Roe v. Wade involved state law, its principles obviously were applicable also to the federal government which had laws against abortion in the territories and the District of Columbia. We find the situation *before* the decision of Roe v. Wade represented by the dotted vertical line dividing liberty from governmental power and the situation *after* Roe v. Wade by the solid line dividing liberty from governmental power. The Court, by its decision, has enlarged constitutional liberty and shrunk governmental power:

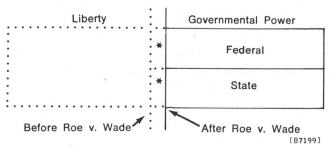

[B7199]

The immediate observation demanded is that this action itself which was taken by the Court, with its clearly defined impact upon the interpretation and application of the Constitution, was not necessarily radical, new, and unheard of. The critical questions which are valid in evaluating any such case are two in number:

(1) On the merits of the particular case of Roe v. Wade, should liberty be defined to include this right of abortion in a pregnant woman? This is a very difficult question about which reasonable people can differ, and members of the Supreme Court did differ. But this question is no different from any question that evaluates the holding of the Court in a constitutional case. Did the Court make the right decision? In the difficult cases, each person answers, sometimes "yes," and sometimes "no." No one agrees with all of the constitutional decisions of the Supreme Court.

[*80*]

These disagreements certainly are not at all surprising because many of the decisions themselves are made by closely divided votes of the justices on the Court.

(2) How free should the Court feel to ignore its prior holdings or the prior accepted scope of liberty or of governmental power when presented with cases raising those questions? Here the Court itself has taken a position contrary to what would normally be expected to be the accepted principle. One might think that a written Constitution is to be strong and rigid and virtually unchangeable. Yet the Court, well over a century ago, began to overrule its prior constitutional decisions and has continued to do so right down to the present time. Indeed, the Court has said specifically that it feels more freedom to overrule a prior constitutional decision once it is convinced that the prior principle is wrong than it feels in changing the interpretations of mere statutes or other legal principles which do not raise constitutional issues. Smith v. Allwright, 321 U.S. 649, 665 (1944). This seemingly illogical position is justified by the Court on the ground that laws are easily changed by legislative enactment, but that the Constitution is difficult to amend. So, when the Court realizes that an earlier principle is wrong, the Court asserts that it must exercise the power to change it.

[*81*]

This recognition of a power to overrule a prior constitutional case does not answer the question of how free the Court should feel to do so. Some people have criticized the Supreme Court in recent years for its seeming willingness to ignore the wisdom of the past and to assume that past decisions are worthy of at most a casual glance.

There is no firm answer to this question. In general, we can only trust the Supreme Court justices to exercise a reasonable measure of self-restraint. They should not intrude their own subjective ideas without humility. They ought to be unwilling to wield the bludgeon upon the earlier constitutional rule when valid doubt as to its current inadequacy exists.

The clearest kinds of cases which show the propriety of the Court changing constitutional interpretation as it feels liberties must be redefined and more broadly protected are the cases involving criminal procedures. Much of the Bill of Rights is directed specifically at fair criminal procedures because of their overwhelming ultimate importance to liberty. But in addition to these specific provisions of the Bill of Rights, the phrase "due process of law," in its more technical meaning, by the use of the word "process" refers specifically to the procedures and processes of law—in brief, to fair trials.

In 1966, the Supreme Court handed down the controversial case of Miranda v. Arizona, 384 U.S. 436. This is the leading case establishing rigid protections for those who are arrested. Persons taken into custody may not be questioned before they are told of their rights. The *"Miranda* warnings," as they have come to be known, require that before anyone is questioned as a suspect about a criminal offense he or she must be warned (1) that anything said by the suspect may be used against him in court, (2) that there is a right to remain silent and not answer any questions, and (3) that the suspect has the right to have a lawyer present and to consult a lawyer during questioning, and if the accused cannot afford to obtain a lawyer, a lawyer will be supplied by the government.

For our purposes, the critical aspect of this holding is that the Court recognized it was creating new and specific standards to govern the questioning of suspects, standards which had not been in existence before. These standards, nevertheless, were found to be constitutionally required under the due process of law clauses of the Fifth and Fourteenth Amendments. Here again, then, the Court was enlarging the area of liberty and cutting down the area of governmental power.

But long before Miranda v. Arizona was decided, the Court had expressed its views on changing notions of fairness in judicial procedures. Half a century ago, Chief Justice Stone said, "The Constitution * * * did not crystallize into changeless form the procedure of 1789." Nashville, C. & St. L. Ry. v. Wallace, 288 U.S. 249, 264 (1933).

There is strong justification for this flexible approach in constitutional law. The concept of due process of law developed in England as a part of the common law. The underlying rationale of the common law is that it is judge-made law which changes and adapts as the needs of society call for it to change and adapt. Thus, "due process of law" was a changing concept in the law long before it was written into the United States Constitution. So the framers of the Constitution were writing into that document a principle of change and adaptation when they put in the phrase "due process of law." Due process did not have then, nor has it ever had since, a firm and fixed content demanding a "literal" constitutional principle. There is, therefore, in the Constitution itself clear justification for recognizing that constitutional concepts of fairness, and more broadly of liberty, properly can change as society in its growth and under new circumstances recognizes meaningful new demands in the protection of human freedom.

The representation of the *Miranda* case on our diagram is the same as the abortion case, Roe v.

Wade. Until that decision, it was not necessary for the government to give all of the warnings to a suspect being questioned in a criminal case. Before the *Miranda* decision, the asterisks were on the side of governmental power. After the decision, they fall in the area of liberty. Again, the Court has moved the dividing line between governmental power and liberty to broaden the area of liberty and restrict the area of governmental power.

So also it is with other familiar decisions of the last few years which recognize a new sweep to personal liberty against the claim of governmental power. These include the cases involving the elimination of racial and sex discrimination, and the elimination of long residence requirements with regard to the right to vote and in the right to use state educational facilities and the right to receive state welfare. Other recent holdings granting new and expanded liberties include the one-person, one-vote principle, and also new protections of free speech against enjoining publications and against claims of defamation.

2. Freedom of Expression ·

The analysis of cases in the all-important freedom of speech situation is aided by the use of our diagram. Beginning with the case of Schenck v. United States, 249 U.S. 47 (1919), Justice Oliver Wendell Holmes, Jr., developed a guiding principle still used today in applying the protection of free speech to those who engage in revolutionary talk or in advocacy of the defiance of valid state and federal law. This principle has come to be known as the "clear and present danger" test. Without going into the nuances of the latest cases, it has reached its modern fruition in the case of Dennis v. United States, 341 U.S. 494 (1951). This is the case that involved the criminal prosecution under the Smith Act for subversive activity of the top officers of the U. S. Communist Party.

The "clear and present danger" test is used in deciding cases involving subversive or radical advocacy. Its import is that we tolerate such advocacy as part of free speech in our constitutional system unless the advocacy creates a "clear and present danger" that it will bring about serious social disruption. In other words, it is not within the power of our federal or state governments to outlaw in all instances even advocacy of the overthrow of the government by force and violence. Such extreme advocacy is constitutionally protected free speech unless the advocacy results in causing a "clear and present danger" that it will bring about social violence, or an actual attempt to overthrow the government by force.

In analyzing these cases in terms of our diagram, the line between liberty and governmental power is drawn on the basis of the clear and present danger principle. Whether the case falls in the area of liberty or in the area of governmental power depends upon whether a clear and present danger exists that the advocacy will bring about these serious evils which the state has a right to prevent. In our diagram, this means that the dividing line is based upon the Court's conclusion concerning whether there exists a clear and present danger from the advocacy. If no clear and present danger is found, then our case involving subversive advocacy falls on the side of liberty and is represented by the numeral ①. If clear and present danger is found, then our case falls on the side of governmental power where the numeral ② is shown. Since the control of subversive speech is almost entirely in the hands of the federal government, our opposition between liberty and governmental power when the subject matter is subversive advocacy is shown in our diagram at the federal level:

Liberty	Governmental Power
①	② Federal
	State

In a subversive advocacy case, this line is stated in terms of "clear and present danger."

[B7200]

In the case of Dennis v. United States, the trial court judge made the decision that the advocacy constituted a clear and present danger. In other words, the determination was made by the court as a "question of law." Justice Douglas, dissenting in that case, said: "I had assumed that the question of the clear and present danger, being so critical an issue in the case, would be a matter for submission to the jury. * * * The Court, I think, errs when it treats the question as one of law."

Was the majority correct on this point in the *Dennis* case or was Justice Douglas correct? Look at our diagram. Who decides constitutional issues? Do we submit constitutional questions to a jury or are our constitutional liberties a question of law for decision by the courts? Stated in another way, should a jury have the power to establish the line dividing liberty and governmental power? In deciding this issue, it should be remembered that if the jury has the power to establish the line, it has the power to move the line in either direction. This would mean that the jury could find that there was a clear and present danger, even though a court did not think so, as well as find there was not a clear and present danger, even though a court did think so.

In other words, looking at our diagram, if we allow this question to be decided by the jury, we

can have a case in which the jury could move the
line to the left to engulf an advocacy in the area
of liberty and put it in the area of governmental
power, as the diagram indicates:

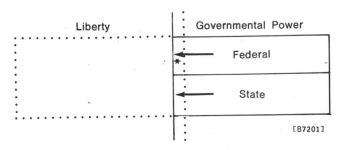

The only way to avoid this dangerous power in
the jury would be to say that the jury has the
power to increase the scope of liberty but not to
decrease it. Logical constitutional analysis, however, fails to justify any such one-way jury power.

Looking at the nature of the constitutional
analysis as demonstrated by our diagram in these
cases, it becomes virtually impossible to escape
the conclusion that the majority of the Court was
correct in the *Dennis* case. We cannot allow a
jury, unskilled in the law and the meaning of the
Constitution and the importance of protecting
constitutional liberty, to make the basic and fundamental constitutional decision in such cases. If
we submitted the issue of clear and present dan-

ger to the jury, that is exactly what we would be doing because it is the clear and present danger principle which defines the area of liberty and the area of governmental power.

Thus, analysis by means of the diagram leads us to the answer most certainly correct in this case. We do not submit the constitutionality of subversive speech to a jury; we submit only the issue of "what happened" to the jury. The most critical of all constitutional decisions is to draw the line between governmental power and liberty. And, as we have already seen in all the cases so far discussed, drawing this line is for the Court.

3. Obscenity and Jury Verdicts

So we have concluded with confidence that we cannot allow constitutionality of an exercise of free speech to turn upon the decision of a jury. Yet we move now into an analysis of one liberty question concerning which, under recent decisions of the Supreme Court, we do allow the jury to draw the line. Our analysis will show that we create a host of problems when we do this. The question for analysis is obscenity, a term which is virtually impossible to define and control.

The problem might be eased somewhat if obscenity were limited to prohibiting indulgence in what society views as seriously anti-social activities. For example, it is still generally accepted that society can prohibit total nudity in public on the streets and in the parks and can prohibit overt sexual activity in public places. This is not because such activity is "wrong conduct," but because the ordinarily private activity is occurring in a public place. Persons have no constitutional right to force exposure of such conduct upon others who do not wish to be exposed to this activity. And such activity or conduct contains very little by way of *advocacy* in the realm of ideas which we have come to think of as protected free speech. This is not to say that it is totally devoid of such advocacy, but the advocacy element is a relatively limited one. Obscenity, however, can become inextricably interwoven with advocacy. The advocacy can be advocacy of sexual freedom, or the advocacy can be political advocacy. Consider an extreme example of a few years ago. A local decision was made in a southern state that a children's book was obscene. The book involved a romance between a rabbit with white fur and a rabbit with black fur. The decision was obviously based upon racial attitudes and had nothing to do with obscenity in the sense in which we would normally view it. To most people, this decision was ridiculous. We can feel confident that the Supreme Court would easily take care of it.

Nevertheless it was not too many years ago that the state of New York refused to allow the showing of the motion picture *Lady Chatterly's Lover,* even though it was a quality motion picture involving no actual depiction of sexual activity. It was "censored" simply because it showed adultery as acceptable conduct in certain circumstances, just as the classic novel by D. H. Lawrence had done. Kingsley Int'l Pictures Corp. v. Regents, 360 U.S. 684 (1959), reversed the New York decision and held the censorship unconstitutional. Here was clear censorship of ideas under the guise of censorship of obscenity. On analysis New York's action was as threatening to the freedom of ideas as was the censorship of the children's book.

There is no need here to detail the struggles which the Supreme Court has gone through in the late years in attempting to deal with the concept of obscenity. Some of that history will be related immediately ahead in another connection. Let the "law" be summarized simply by saying that it now appears that obscenity is limited to the portrayal of explicit sexual matters and whether a publication is obscene or not depends upon "local community standards" as decided by a jury.

It is easy to develop sympathy for this current conclusion by the Supreme Court. If it were otherwise, says the Court, the Court itself would have to serve as the censoring body for the entire nation. The Court would have to decide as a question of law whether any particular publication is obscene or not. In addition, this would mean that the Court would have to read or look at everything which is charged with being obscene to make the final constitutional decision.

But leaving the matter to local juries is an even more dangerous solution. Shortly after the Supreme Court decided that the issue of obscenity should be submitted to a jury, a jury in Georgia found the award-winning movie *Carnal Knowledge* obscene. This was too much for the Supreme Court. It reversed the case, Jenkins v. Georgia, 418 U.S. 153 (1974), just as it had done earlier in the case of *Lady Chatterly's Lover*. This particular movie, the Court held, could not possibly be obscene even though a jury had said that it was. So even though the Court tries to avoid being the ultimate decision-maker on obscenity, one may be forced to go all the way to the Supreme Court to vindicate a free speech right in a motion picture.

But even this is not the major problem in allowing the issue of obscenity to be submitted to a jury on a standard of local community attitudes. The most troublesome result of the Court's current analysis is that a book or magazine with na-

[*93*]

tion-wide circulation may be constitutionally privileged free speech in many communities, but may be obscene in others. The publisher can be found guilty of a criminal offense for publishing material which in most places in the United States is constitutionally privileged free speech.

The fallacy of this approach is revealed by our analysis. We have already shown the fallacy of having the dividing line between constitutional liberty and governmental power drawn by a jury. A person's freedom should not be dependent upon the unskilled views of local jurors. Giving this power to the jury gives the jury the power to interpret the Constitution—to decide issues of constitutional law.

But there is an even more serious fallacy. A publication for nation-wide circulation is subject to being found obscene by a local jury and its author and publisher are sent to jail. Yet, in other communities, for example, where the material was published, it is not just lawful but is constitutionally privileged speech. The point is that our diagram shows that if the community is one, even under the Supreme Court's definition of obscenity, in which the particular publication is lawful, that means that it is constitutionally protected free speech. It is not merely "permitted" by law.

This important point may seem to be confusing and obscure. But it can be better understood by going back in the history of the Supreme Court's handling of obscenity to an earlier faulty analysis which still persists in this peculiar current rule.

The faulty analysis began not in an obscenity case but in a case involving a "group libel" law, Beauharnais v. Illinois, 343 U.S. 250 (1952). The issue in this case was whether a statute which made criminal any statements exposing "the citizens of any race, color, creed, or religion to contempt, derision, or obloquy * * * " fell within the area of state governmental power or within the area of constitutionally privileged speech. The majority of the Court held that such statements were not constitutionally protected as free speech. The curiosity is in the analysis of Justice Frankfurter writing for the Court. He reasoned that this statute was one prohibiting libel and, therefore, there was no free speech issue.

The grave difficulty with this reasoning was that this was not a libel statute within any of the prior instances of libel statutes. This was not a state's prohibition of private criticism by one person of another person, but was a prohibition of political advocacy that went beyond the bounds of what the state defined as acceptable limits. In effect the Court said that because we call this a libel statute (although it was not a typical libel statute), we, therefore, have no free speech ques-

[*95*]

tion and we need not evaluate the statute on a free speech basis.

This approach shows that the Court totally overlooked the fact that in every case involving speech the issue is the opposition of governmental power to the claims of constitutional liberty. Merely categorizing this statute as prohibiting libel does not remove the constitutional issue of whether it falls in the area of liberty. In fact, categorizing the statute as a libel statute assumes the answer to the very issue raised.

That the reasoning of the Court in the *Beauharnais* case was erroneous was made quite clear some years later by the Supreme Court in the leading case of New York Times Co. v. Sullivan, 376 U.S. 254 (1964). This case placed most stringent restrictions upon laws establishing the right to sue for libel under the justification that in libel cases there is a critical concern for the protection of free speech.

This same approach—if we call it libel then we don't have to worry about the free speech implications—arose again in defining obscenity. The early leading modern case is Roth v. United States, 354 U.S. 476 (1957). This case involved a typical state statute outlawing the publication of obscene printed matter. Justice Brennan, speaking for the Court, said: "The dispositive question is whether obscenity is utterance within the area of protected speech and press." Then, Justice Brennan, quoting from the *Beauharnais* case, denied that there should be a use of any free speech test. Instead, the Court just said again that obscenity is not protected speech, and the complete answer is, following the reasoning of the *Beauharnais* holding, that anything falling into the classification of obscenity cannot be protected free speech.

The trouble with this analysis is, of course, that it puts the question in reverse. The Court classifies a particular publication as obscene or libelous and by that means avoids deciding the issue of whether it falls within the scope of constitutionally protected speech. Referring to our diagram, the Court seemed unwilling to face the issue that regulating obscenity or defamation raises a free speech and liberty question. Yet, it is obvious that the constitutionality of the regulation must be faced in those terms. The only way one can decide that censorship of a particular publication is constitutionally permissible is to decide that it does not fall in the area of liberty. This decision cannot be justified simply by calling it a name—obscene or libelous. The issue of constitutional liberty must be faced.

The only adequate analysis is that speech by anyone is free unless there is constitutional justification for the state to be able to stop it. The justification cannot be found by labelling it. It can only be found by evaluating whether or not it is speech which the Constitution intended to preserve as free. In our diagram, the issue is whether the case falls in the area of liberty or in the area of governmental power to control. The only way to decide that issue is to place the considerations demanding freedom—①— against the considerations demanding governmental power—②.

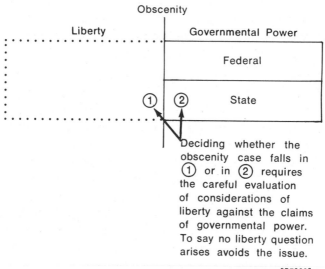

Obscenity

Liberty   Governmental Power

Federal

① ②   State

Deciding whether the obscenity case falls in ① or in ② requires the careful evaluation of considerations of liberty against the claims of governmental power. To say no liberty question arises avoids the issue.

[B7202]

Labelling something "obscene" can be justified only as the statement of the result after the constitutional evaluation has been made. In the *Roth* case, the Court used the name as an epithet to reach the result without the evaluation.

Justice Brennan recognizing that he had been in error has abandoned the approach he wrote into the earlier *Roth* case. Paris Adult Theatre I v. Slaton, 413 U.S. 49, 73 (1973) (dissenting opinion). In addition as mentioned above, the recent case of New York Times Co. v. Sullivan has openly shown that the Court now evaluates the governmental power to control defamation against a strong and firm recognition of the liberty element in utterances that might be charged as libelous.

Back again to the issue of leaving to a jury the ultimate question as to whether a publication is obscene. We see clearly that we are in actuality asking the jury to place considerations of liberty against considerations of governmental power to determine whether someone will go to the penitentiary or not. This is no more a traditional jury function in our system than is the determination of whether there is a "clear and present danger," or whether freedom of religion includes the right of polygamous marriages. The job of the jury is to find the facts—to find what happened —not to find whether a particular action is offensive to public order, safety, or morals. This kind of judgment is a policy decision to be made by the legislature in its criminal statutes and against the background of the protections of constitutional liberty.

As mentioned above, shortly after the Supreme Court decided to try to leave questions concerning obscenity to the jury, their new approach was effectively weakened by the necessity of having to overrule a jury verdict from Georgia that the motion picture *Carnal Knowledge* was obscene. At least the Court has recognized that it will allow the jury to act only in a limited area in deciding whether a particular publication is obscene.

Let us put the analysis of our current law on obscenity, whether satisfactory or not, on our diagram. Remember that the diagram is now being applied only to the obscenity issue, because only in this situation do we allow the jury to make a constitutional decision. The two solid lines would show the Court's outer limits on the leeway they would allow a jury in drawing a line. If the case under analysis is represented either as number ① or number ③ below, this would mean that the Court was insisting itself that the decision was in the area of liberty—①—or in the area of the governmental power to control—③. But if the Court decides that the case falls in the small "buffer" zone—number ②—the Court would leave it to the jury to decide whether the case involved constitutionally protected liberty or acceptable governmental exercise of power to control:

Arguably there is some justification for allowing such a question to go to the jury. We recognize that we do submit to the jury certain "mixed questions of law and fact" which allow the jury within narrow limits to draw legal conclusions based upon the facts. The concept of "negligence" in automobile accidents is such a concept. The jury is allowed to decide not only what actually happened in the accident, but also whether a driver was "negligent" or not. We restrict this jury power within narrow limits by reserving to courts the right to reverse a decision where the courts decide that the jury's conclusion on the mixed question of law and fact is erroneous "as a matter of law." This, in effect, is exactly what

[*101*]

the Supreme Court did in the case involving the motion picture *Carnal Knowledge*.

But this current state of the law is particularly troublesome and, indeed, unacceptable for two reasons. The first is the fact that we send people who have published a book or a magazine to prison based upon a jury's decision that the particular publication was locally obscene—that it did not fall in the area of constitutionally protected speech. These are not the kinds of questions we submit to juries in criminal cases where we ask the jury to decide only what happened. But even more serious is the fact that inevitably, as was mentioned above, this current Court rule on obscenity means that publications sold nation-wide are constitutionally privileged free speech in some parts of the country but their publication is a criminal offense elsewhere. We have already seen the spectre of overzealous prosecutors deciding locally to prosecute publishers or participants in nation-wide publications or nationally distributed motion pictures. While a local jury-enforced standard of obscenity may have some acceptability as to purely local activities, it simply can have no acceptability in the case of nation-wide publication.

At this point, some readers may feel that there is something faulty or lacking in this analysis which opposes the Supreme Court's handling of obscenity. Different communities have differing laws concerning the sale of liquor, the closing hour of taverns, the sale of merchandise on Sunday, gambling, and the like. We do not have nation-wide standards as to these matters. As you go from one community to another, you must be careful to obey the laws of that community concerning these other matters.

This valid local diversity must be carefully and completely distinguished from local diversity with regard to libel and obscenity. As we have seen from our diagram, libel and obscenity are subject to the control of governmental power only on the basis of a determination that these publications are not constitutionally protected free speech. In the other instances mentioned here, there is no serious liberty issue. There is no constitutional right to gamble; the state is free to allow gambling or forbid it. Either the tolerance of gambling or the outlawing of gambling falls in the area of governmental power. The same discretion to exercise power or not is given to government under a specific holding of the Court with respect to the right to prohibit businesses selling the usual run of merchandise on Sunday. Braunfeld v. Brown, 366 U.S. 599 (1961). The same power is given with respect to the control of the sale of alcoholic beverages and the closing hour of taverns.

[*103*]

These are all instances where the state is free to control or not as it wishes. There is governmental power to make either choice. So these issues fall wholly on the right-hand side of our diagram and do not to any serious extent involve issues of constitutional liberty. These controls of individual conduct are simply comparable in constitutional analysis to a reasonable speed limit, parking regulations, zoning regulations, law regulating the registration of securities or the registration of lobbyists, and many others. On the other hand, the failure of a state to pass laws prohibiting murder, or theft, rape, and other serious crimes might well be a constitutional violation of the liberty of its citizens through the state's unwillingness to protect against those serious crimes to the person. But the great mass of general governmental regulation does not fall in this category.

In our diagram, gambling, zoning, the sale of liquor, Sunday sales, and the like fall unquestionably on the side of governmental power, so there is no serious constitutional issue as it relates to liberty. The only real question constitutionally in such general regulation today is whether the power falls in the area of national or state power. This will be the subject of detailed consideration with the use of the diagram in Chapters 5 and 6.

4. Competing Constitutional Liberties

We continue our analysis of particular situations in constitutional liberty by turning now to the common situation of two claimed constitutional liberties which compete with each other. The problem raised here is most easily seen in racial, religious, and sex discrimination. There is a constitutional liberty of broad extent and significant impact to be free from discrimination based upon race and other similar classifications. Racial discriminations and some others are "invidious," as the Court calls them. This means, as stated on page 69, that they are unconstitutional unless some compelling state interest is shown. Discriminations in the quality of schools, in voting rights, in residence requirements, and in the use of public facilities are also constitutionally outlawed.

There is, however, a rarely mentioned constitutional right to discriminate on the basis of race, religion, and other similar classifications. Consider the right of the individual in marriage to discriminate on the basis of race or any other basis in choosing a life mate. There is undoubtedly a constitutional right to engage in discrimination in various kinds of private associations.

This right to discriminate is valid even though we now have so broadened the Thirteenth

Amendment that we find it outlaws even some private discriminations on a racial basis as "badges of slavery." The Court has held that private schools fulfilling the public compulsory education function may not discriminate on a racial basis, Runyon v. McCrary, 427 U.S. 160 (1976), and has held that private citizens in selling their real property may not discriminate on a racial basis. Jones v. Alfred H. Mayer Co., 392 U.S. 409 (1968).

The critical constitutional issue posed is whether the protection against discrimination, especially in the racial area where private racial discriminations are outlawed by the Thirteenth Amendment, is too great an infringement upon a private right to discriminate on a racial basis, at least in family and personal relationships. To understand this issue, let us use for a moment another diagram which later will be incorporated into our basic diagram. This is a simple line diagram that shows the constitutional freedom from discrimination placed in opposition to the constitutional right to discriminate. Let us assume that this line diagram is referring to racial situations. All that this line diagram attempts to show is that as we move away from the obvious situations where racial discrimination is prohibited by the Constitution, we move toward situations where the individual may have a constitutional right to discriminate on a racial basis, as in the home and in choosing personal friends and companions and so on:

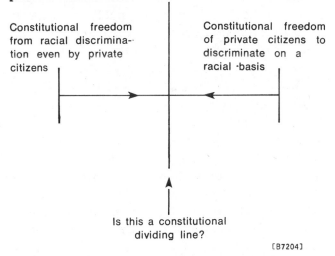

Constitutional freedom from racial discrimination even by private citizens

Constitutional freedom of private citizens to discriminate on a racial basis

Is this a constitutional dividing line?

[B7204]

The question posed by this diagram is whether the constitutional right to be free from racial discrimination even by private citizens runs directly up against the constitutional right of private citizens to discriminate on a racial basis at a fixed and firm dividing line. Or restating the same question, is there an area in the middle where the state has some power either to permit or to prohibit discrimination by private citizens? If so, the two competing constitutional rights would not run abruptly against each other, and there would be an area which falls neither in the constitution-

[*107*]

al right to discriminate nor the constitutional freedom from discrimination.

The answer to this question at the moment is clearly that there is an area in between the rights of individuals to discriminate and not to be discriminated against and in this area the government can permit or outlaw discrimination as it wishes. As we shall see later, there is no holding by the Supreme Court that makes it unconstitutional for someone in business to discriminate on a racial basis with respect to the employees hired or the customers served. The fact that we outlaw racial discrimination in these situations under the Civil Rights Act of 1964 is an exercise of governmental power to outlaw or not outlaw such discrimination as the government wishes.

Another example showing that there is an intermediate area where there is governmental power to permit or outlaw racial and similar discriminations concerns private clubs. Moose Lodge v. Irvis, 407 U.S. 163 (1972), held that the lodge could discriminate on a racial basis. Yet the Court assumes that a private club which sets itself up as a relatively large and important commercial enterprise, as Moose Lodge did, probably could be forbidden to discriminate on a racial basis if by legislative policy we wish to do so.

Thus, the line diagram immediately above is not accurate. Rather, the true situation is that there is a constitutional freedom from racial discrimination and a constitutional right to discriminate, but there is also an area of legislative policy between the two rights. In this middle area by legislation we can outlaw racial discrimination or we can allow it. Thus, the more accurate diagram looks like this:

Constitutional freedom from racial discrimination by private citizens

Constitutional freedom of private citizens to discriminate on a racial basis

Area of governmental power to make policy concerning racial discrimination by allowing it or prohibiting it

[B7205]

Where constitutional liberties are involved, it is becoming increasingly common to think automatically in terms of absolutes—that the Constitution covers all issues. It is important, therefore, to recognize that we allow the exercise of governmental power with respect to many matters that touch deeply on issues of liberty; and the reason we do so is because there are competing liberties. The reconciliation of these competing interests in liberty by way of policy decisions where the Constitution does not control is an important function of a democratic government.

Let us now put our simple line diagram into our basic analytical diagram to remove any confusion that might arise from shifting to another approach. The simple line diagram was used merely to dramatize the direct opposition to each other that competing constitutional liberties can have. For clarity we leave out the line dividing federal and state power because it is irrelevant at this point. In our simple line diagram, we have merely drawn a progression from one constitutional right to another; both of these constitutional rights are located on the liberty side of our basic diagram. The middle area on the line diagram which represents governmental policy-making power is located on the governmental power side of our basic diagram:

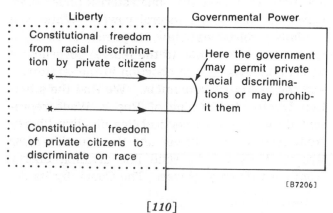

You will notice we have simply taken the straight line diagram and turned it back on itself so that it fits our basic analysis.

The exercise of the governmental power to lean either toward constitutional freedom from discrimination or constitutional freedom to discriminate is clearly shown in the Civil Rights Act of 1964. The clear thrust of that statute is to create new nonconstitutional freedoms from discrimination with respect to hiring practices and the service of customers in businesses. Yet the statute does not cover all businesses, and insofar as it contains exemptions, it is leaning toward the constitutional freedom to discriminate. The specific exception of private clubs in the Civil Rights Act of 1964 is one such example.

Although we tend not to think of a minimum voting age as a discrimination, it is one of the clearest examples in our society of discrimination. The voting age used to be 21 as set by statutes. But by the Twenty-Sixth Amendment it has now been made 18. There is nothing in the Constitution which prohibits a state from setting the voting age at 17. The state is free to set the voting age below 18 if it wishes to do so, just as some states had set the voting age below 21 when 21 was the accepted norm. Yet, it is only reasonable to expect that there is a voting age below which the state would not be allowed to go because the age would obviously be unreasonably and irrationally low. A constitutional right in candidates and in the populace generally to be free from the influence of the voting of young children would be recognized as part of a right to vote. So we have here another example of a range of governmental power to make policy decisions between the limits of two competing constitutional rights.

Let us remind ourselves that the Constitution does not solve all problems concerning what may happen to an individual in our society. Over and over again this fact comes as a shock to many who, without clear analysis, feel that all of the protection of their freedoms, from whatever source assailed, must be found in the Constitution. We even tend to overlook the fact that it is the state criminal laws which protect the most overwhelmingly important aspects of our freedom —life and property.

In the last few years, there have been three decisions of the United States Supreme Court which are particularly disturbing to some persons who do not remind themselves of the fact that constitutionally protected liberties do not cover the entire range of important personal rights. The best known of these cases is Paul v. Davis, 424 U.S. 693 (1976). This case involved a suit against the Louisville, Kentucky, police chief claiming that the police chief had violated Davis' civil rights by circulating a confidential flyer to local stores listing him as an "active shoplifter," although he had never been convicted of shoplifting. The Court held that Davis had no constitutional right to be protected against this circulation, because the government took no legally cognizable action of any kind against him. There could be a personal remedy by suing Police Chief Paul for damages for defamation or suing the city for a tort under a tort claims act, but no constitutional right was violated.

During the same term of Court, we also have Bishop v. Wood, 426 U.S. 341 (1976), which held that a policeman did not have any constitutional right to a hearing before being discharged. It did not deny the right of a policeman to bring suit for wrongful discharge later. If there were a right to a pretermination hearing, it had to be found in the employment contract which the policeman had with his employer—the city. In other words, the due process of law clause did not mandate a pretermination hearing; the city had the right either to provide or not provide it.

Similar analyses have been found in cases involving prisoners who sue to protest the failure to give hearings before transfers or other actions are taken which may place them in less favorable situations. The Court has held that the Constitution does not require full hearings before taking such actions. Montanye v. Haymes, 427 U.S. 236 (1976).

As has been pointed out above, many of our most fundamental liberties are dependent upon legislation—the protection against being murdered or against having our property stolen. What bothers those who are concerned about these cases, and there is an extensive literature of opposition to the decision in Paul v. Davis particularly, is that they do not agree with them. But they imply that Davis should not be listed on a known shoplifters' bulletin whether or not this right is constitutionally protected, that a policeman should have a right to a hearing before being discharged whether or not the Constitution requires it, and that prisoners should have the right to a hearing before they are moved from one prison to another or one situation to another.

The Court held that whether or not there should be such rights, these were not constitutional rights. There is no question but that these "rights" can be protected by legislation if the state wishes to do so. It can give the policeman the right to a hearing if it wishes; it can give the prisoner the right to a hearing if it wishes; it can prohibit the circulation of a shoplifters' list if it wishes. But the Court was holding only that the Constitution does not protect against these actions. And the Court had no power to hold that state policy should be otherwise.

The danger in too broad a constitutional requirement is that every action of the state that is detrimental to someone then is found to infringe upon a constitutional liberty. What is overlooked in such a conclusion is that virtually every state action taken, which disadvantages somebody, advantages somebody else. Thus listing possible shoplifters advantages businessmen, discharging police without full hearings in advance saves time and taxpayers' money, not holding a hearing every time action is taken against a prisoner saves much time and cost and makes easier the enforcement of discipline in penal institutions. Such actions, therefore, should be evaluated first on the basis of constitutional liberty, but then if no constitutional liberty is found, it should be understood that there simply remains the right of the government as a matter of policy to engage or not to engage in such activity and that there is no longer a question concerning constitutional "liberty."

Liberties can be created by legislation; witness the Civil Rights Act of 1964. But then these are not constitutional liberties. The analysis of our diagram makes clear that the issue of liberty in our Constitution is set in opposition to the issue of governmental power. Once it is determined that no constitutional liberty is infringed, as was the situation in the cases mentioned above, then as far as the Constitution is concerned, the state is free, as a policy matter, to act in accordance with the democratic processes of decision. But to call the results of that action either "liberty" or a denial of "liberty" is to shift from analyzing constitutional liberty to making value judgments on various policies.

A 30 mile an hour speed limit infringes upon the liberty of those who can drive safely at 35. The new minimum wage escalating to $3.35 by 1981 infringes upon the liberty of those who are inept as employees and are willing to work for less than that amount, but can't get jobs at the minimum wage. A prohibition against the use of Laetrile in treating cancer infringes upon the liberty of those who wish to use it. The granting of a TV license to one applicant infringes upon the liberty of a rival applicant to own and operate a TV station, and of potential listeners who would prefer a station operated by the other applicant. But none of these are constitutional liberty issues; they simply reflect the policy decisions which must be made in any society once we find there is no constitutional liberty.

You may well feel that Paul v. Davis, Bishop v. Wood, and Montayne v. Haymes are incorrectly decided. But if this is your belief, it must be based upon a conclusion that there should be a *constitutional* right of a policeman to have a hearing before being discharged, a *constitutional* right not to be listed on a known shoplifters' list for restricted circulation without having a prior conviction or a hearing, and a *constitutional* right for a prisoner to have a hearing before being transferred. You cannot properly believe constitutional analysis in such a case is wrong as a "policy" matter. Policy is for the legislature. It should be recognized that the state is free to grant hearings in all of those cases if it wishes to do so, even though, as the Court held, there is no constitutional compulsion to grant hearings.

5. Conclusion

This chapter of analysis will be ended on a note of caution. We protect against racial discrimination by government in many aspects of our lives. Under the Thirteenth Amendment we even protect against *private* racial discriminations. But even in the situation of racial discrimination by the government, there are no absolutes. Open and blatant racial discrimination in governmental actions can be constitutionally justified in certain situations. May the President choose among possibilities for an ambassador to a black African nation on the basis of race? I should think so, without any question. May the President carefully exclude from consideration all persons of Arab national origin in choosing an envoy to Israel? Again, there should be no doubt. Yet these are instances of governmental discrimination on a racial or national origin basis.

This kind of situation is not the only one in which the government can discriminate on these otherwise improper bases. Should a President be entitled to choose cabinet members and other high government appointees taking such matters as race, religion, and sex into account? I should clearly think so.

The question of whether to allow benign quotas as against reverse discrimination in certain situations is a very difficult one. And the Supreme Court may be speaking on this issue shortly. But these matters are mentioned here only as the capstone to an analysis of constitutional liberty to stress that the law does not abide in absolutes. Even constitutional principles are matters of degree and balance and depend upon the particular situation and the particular circumstances which are involved. Accordingly, the determination of constitutionality through judicial decision is very important to and so effective in our system. The courts deal only with cases; they deal only with particular situations. A sterile principle of constitutionality is meaningless until it is applied, and it is in the application that the scope of our freedoms is to be found.

CHAPTER 4

CONGRESSIONAL PROTECTION OF CONSTITUTIONAL LIBERTIES

1. The Political Protection of Constitutional Liberty

We turn our attention to the role that Congress plays in protecting constitutional liberties. In doing so we must note that the role of the President and the executive departments is an outgrowth of the congressional protection of liberty. In domestic as opposed to foreign matters, with only rare and narrow exceptions, the President acts only under the statutory authorizations of Congress. Thus, the major role that the Department of Health, Education, and Welfare has played in eliminating racial discrimination in schools and in other public activities has been a role authorized and established by the legislation of Congress.

The subject matter of this chapter was briefly described in Chapter 2 at page 52. The analysis of constitutional liberty has been presented as protecting the rights of the individual against governmental intrusion. Most of our constitutional liberties are of this nature. Yet, the power of the person to confront the government is useless without legal strength to back the person's claim. And legal strength can come only from the government.

The classic confrontation in constitutional liberty, therefore, is the individual citizen backed by the courts, the judicial branch of government, against the other branches of the government which are trying to regulate and control the citizen in ways that the Constitution forbids. Technically, therefore, the confrontation is government against government with the courts protecting the individual citizen, or the small minority group of citizens, against the democratic processes which can properly be said to represent in an inexact way the majority view of the people.

The critical point is, of course, that there must be orderly legal process strong enough to protect the rights of citizens against governmental intrusion. In our system, this orderly process with the strength to protect comes largely from the courts and the willingness of the other branches of government to accept and support this judicial role.

The significance of this circumstance can be seen by comparing liberty in our country with the frustrating search for liberty in a totalitarian nation, such as the U.S.S.R. The Soviet Constitution contains elaborate protections of individual rights. These protections have no substantial legal significance, however. Soviet citizens cannot claim these rights without having the legal backing of some branch of government. There is no such backing in the Soviet Union, because all branches of government are deeply subservient to the Soviet state. There is no independent strength nor indeed any real concept of independent strength in the courts, when the confrontation is between the citizen and the government. The courts do function, and effectively so, but only when the confrontation is between private citizens without serious governmental concern.

The nature of constitutional liberty in the United States as protected by the courts has probably never been better described in a few words than by Justice Jackson, writing for the Supreme Court, in West Virginia State Board of Education v. Barnette, 319 U.S. 624, 638 (1943):

> "The very purpose of a Bill of Rights was to withdraw certain subjects from the vicissitudes of political controversy, to place them beyond the reach of majorities and officials and to establish them as legal principles to be applied by the courts. One's right to life, liberty, and property, to free speech, a free press, freedom of worship and assembly, and other fundamental rights may not be submitted to vote; they depend on the outcome of no elections."

This classic definition of how constitutional liberty is protected must now be modified to some extent because of recent strong congressional statutory activity in the protection of constitutional liberties, as well as by the Court itself having resurrected some congressional statutes passed at the close of the Civil War, through reversing older decisions. In this chapter, we explore the analytical aspects of this congressional activity directed toward protecting constitutional liberty.

Our starting point is to repeat the diagram as it was presented on page 54 in Chapter 2. The usual pattern in our constitutional structure is for the courts to define and enforce the large area of individual constitutional liberties which has been taken away from governmental power. Yet increasingly in the last few years, with Court approval, the Congress has played a significant role by creating strong and effective statutory remedies both civil and criminal against those who interfere with the individual liberties of citizens. Hence, in our diagram:

Liberty	Governmental Power
	Federal
	State

[B7207]

Enforced and protected in most instances by Court decision, but also protected by the passage of "civil rights" legislation in Congress, and by the President in enforcing court decisions and civil rights legislation.

This enforcement function of the Congress, and the Executive acting under congressional legislation, must be kept analytically separate from the creation by Congress of rights in citizens which look like constitutional liberties but actually are rights created only under the general powers of Congress to legislate. We must be reminded again that the Civil Rights Act of 1964, 42 U.S. C.A. § 2000, in eliminating discrimination on the basis of race and religion in public accommodations, hotels, restaurants, retail stores, and the like, and eliminating racial, religious and sex discrimination in employment practices does not fall on the liberty side of our diagram. These rights of citizens are created wholly by statute out of the general power of Congress to pass laws which affect interstate commerce under Article I, Section 8, of the Constitution.

This power wielded by Congress is exactly of the same nature that the states use in passing the general criminal laws which protect the life and property of individual citizens from intrusion by other private citizens. Also included in this category of laws are all of the general mass of regulatory legislation protecting citizens from, for example, deceitful advertising, interest rates which are too high, or protecting citizens by right-of-way rules in highway traffic, full disclosure laws in the sale of securities, and pure food and drug laws. These laws are all protecting "rights" of citizens in some way. The serious constitutional issue in most of these laws is simply whether they fall within the area of federal or state power, or both.

In contrast, we are concerned here with congressional legislation passed to implement *constitutional* liberties—those rights of the individual which throughout our analysis have fallen in that broad area of rights to be protected against governmental control and regulation.

The origin of this constitutional power is found in the last section of many of the amendments, the most important for constitutional liberties being the Thirteenth and Fourteenth. Congress is given specific power to "enforce" amendments by appropriate legislation.

There is one critical constitutional issue raised by the exercise of this enforcement power by Congress. What is the meaning of the word *enforce*? Does it mean that Congress has the power simply to create criminal and civil penalties for those who violate citizens' rights under the Constitution? Or does it mean that Congress itself can define and determine the scope of constitutional liberties by legislation?

In terms of our diagram, can Congress actually enlarge the scope of liberty under the Constitution? (Or shrink it?) Does enforcement include the right to move the all-powerful dividing line between constitutional liberties and governmental power?

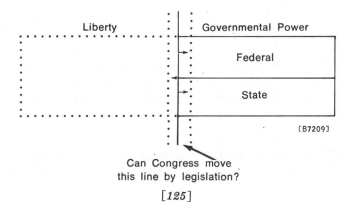

Can Congress move
this line by legislation?

[*125*]

This inquiry is properly stated in these legal terms: Can Congress make some governmental action unconstitutional that is now constitutional under Court decisions defining the scope of constitutional liberty, or can Congress make something which the Court has said now falls in the area of constitutional liberty subject to the exercise of governmental power?

The almost automatic answer to these questions by anyone steeped in the tradition of American constitutionalism would be that the congressional power to enforce is no more than a power to create civil and criminal liability in those persons who infringe the constitutional liberties defined by the Court's interpretation of the Constitution. Our well-settled constitutional concept has been that the Constitution is supreme over congressional law and that mere statutory law cannot alter the scope of constitutional liberty.

The question, however, is not as easily disposed of as might be assumed. The Thirteenth and Fourteenth Amendments were a new departure in constitutionalism. For the first time, broad protection of citizens' liberties against state intrusion was put in the Constitution. For the first time, the amendments adopted the practice, which has since been followed as a routine matter in constitutional amendments, of giving to Congress the power to "enforce * * * by appropriate legislation."

The early history of judicial unwillingness to get involved in defining the scope of the amendments, particularly the Fourteenth Amendment, has been detailed in Chapter 2. The interesting complementary principle was the Court's emphasis upon the congressional power. In Ex Parte Virginia, 100 U.S. 339, decided in 1880, one of the early cases involving the interpretation and application of the Fourteenth Amendment, the Court said that the Thirteenth and Fourteenth Amendments "derive much of their force" from the provision giving Congress the power to enforce the amendment:

> "It is not said the *judicial power* of the general government shall extend to enforcing the prohibitions and to protecting the rights and immunities guaranteed. It is not said that branch of the government shall be authorized to declare void any action of a state in violation of the prohibitions. It is the power of Congress which has been enlarged."

If this view of the Thirteenth and Fourteenth Amendments had prevailed, there would be no question but that the definition of the scope of the liberties of citizens would be largely in the hands of Congress rather than in the hands of the courts. This is a shocking idea to American citizens since we have so thoroughly accepted the concept of judicial review and the judicial definition of the content of citizen liberties. As the discussion in Chapter 2 indicates, this view of a broad congressional role in enforcing the amendments was not accepted.

So the courts originally started with the idea that they had little to do with the responsibilities of protecting the new freedoms found in the Thirteenth and Fourteenth Amendments. But citizen lawsuits kept pressuring them, and the courts gradually yielded to the temptation to take to themselves this great power available to them. So it became routine and accepted that the courts defined the scope of constitutional liberty. Accordingly, Justice Jackson placed the exclusive emphasis upon the judicial protection of liberties in the quotation at page 121 above. In terms of our diagram, the courts and not the Congress draw the critical constitutional dividing line between individual liberty and governmental power.

There is a modern development on this issue. One decision in the United States Supreme Court holds that Congress has the power to expand the scope of constitutional liberty—to move the dividing line between liberty and governmental power to the right so that it shrinks governmental power and increases the breadth of liberty. The development which culminated in this deci-

[*128*]

sion began with the case of Lassiter v. North-hampton Election Board, 360 U.S. 45 (1959). In this case, the Supreme Court upheld the right of a state to maintain an English literacy requirement as a qualification for voters. In other words, there was no constitutional right to vote without minimum required proficiency in English.

In the Voting Rights Act of 1965, Congress outlawed the use of English literacy tests as a qualification for voting for persons who had gone to "American flag" schools (mainly Puerto Ricans). In the case of Katzenbach v. Morgan, 384 U.S. 641 (1966), the Supreme Court upheld the power of Congress to alter the constitutionality of the English literacy test requirement pursuant to its enforcement power under Section 5 of the Fourteenth Amendment. Justice Brennan, writing for the Court, quoted the old case of Ex Parte Virginia and reasoned that the right to enforce the Fourteenth Amendment included the right to make an English literacy test, which the Supreme Court had held constitutional, into an unconstitutional violation of the rights of citizens under the Fourteenth Amendment. In terms of our diagram, this is what happened:

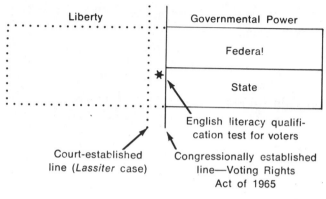

[B7213]

This holding by the Court is troublesome as a general proposition of constitutional law, and it is also troublesome specifically. In a general proposition, it is troublesome because it destroys or at least seriously weakens the core American constitutional principle that the ultimate authority in defining constitutional rights is the judiciary. Specifically, it is troublesome because if the Congress has the power to increase individual liberties, logic demands that it also have the power to decrease them. In terms of our diagram, if Congress can move the critical dividing line between liberty and governmental power to the right, it can also move it to the left.

The dissenting justices in Katzenbach v. Morgan pointed out the unfortunate aspects of a "two-way" power of Congress if a congressional

[*130*]

power to redefine is recognized. The opinion by Justice Brennan, however, disposed of this contention in a footnote simply by saying that Congress' power under Section 5 is limited to adopting measures to enforce the guarantees of the amendment and does not grant Congress the power to restrict, abrogate, or dilute these guarantees.

This brief and casual answer by the Court on this specific problem is simplistic and wholly inadequate. We have already seen that constitutional liberties consist unavoidably of the balancing of the rights of an individual against the rights of other individuals. Every protection of the constitutional freedom of one individual to act a certain way is a denial of the freedom of other citizens not to be subjected to that action or conduct. A constitutional limitation upon the laws against defamation is an intrusion upon the liberties of those who are defamed. Everytime we increase the protections of those accused of crime, we to some extent lessen the protections of the potential victims of crime. By legislation authorizing non-English speaking voters, we are to some extent lessening the voting strength and power of English-speaking voters.

These comparisons are not made to take sides in these situations; they are made simply to indicate the fact that the granting of a constitutional liberty to one person is a lessening of the rights of other people. There is no attempt to say that this consequence is good or bad in a particular situation; it is simply a reality which must be recognized analytically.

So, when Justice Brennan says that Congress can only enlarge liberties and not shrink them, he is saying, in a simplistic way, that Congress can only do what the Court will accept as a strengthening of liberty, but at the same time he is disavowing the power of the Court to make that decision. As Justice Harlan said in his dissent:

> "In effect the Court reads § 5 of the Fourteenth Amendment as giving Congress the power to define the *substantive* scope of the amendment. If that indeed be the true reach of § 5, then I do not see why Congress should not be able as well to exercise its § 5 'discretion' by enacting statutes so as in effect to dilute equal protection and due process decisions of this Court. In all such cases, there is room for reasonable men to differ as to whether or not a denial of equal protection or due process has occurred, and the final decision is one of judgment. Until today, this judgment has always been one for the judiciary to resolve."

The flight of Justice Brennan's trial balloon is one of the shortest in constitutional history. Oregon v. Mitchell, 400 U.S. 112 (1970), involved the Voting Rights Act Amendments of 1970. Part of the amendments lowered the minimum age of voters in both state and federal elections from 21 to 18. There was no real question about the right of Congress to lower the voting age in federal elections. The terms of Article I of the Constitution might appear to cast doubt on the power of Congress simply because the provision defines voter qualifications for federal elections as those qualifications set by the states for their elections. But it has long been accepted as an inherent federal power that the federal government could establish its own qualifications if it found the state qualifications unacceptable.

The critical issue in the case was whether Congress could lower the voting age from 21 to 18 in state as opposed to federal elections. This was a perfect case for the Court again to use the principle of Katzenbach v. Morgan that Congress can redefine the breadth of constitutional liberty. On analysis, that is exactly what Congress had tried to do, just as it had undertaken to do with respect to literacy tests. Congress had tried to force the states to lower the voting age to 18 as a constitutional right for those over 18 to vote in state elections. Yet the majority of the Court refused to accept any rationale that Congress could change the substantive scope of liberty by enacting a law establishing 18 as the constitutional voting age. Justice Brennan's dissent, as you might suppose, was anguished.

Today, then, it must be accepted that the law still is that the courts retain the ultimate authority to define the scope of liberty and governmental power under the Constitution. The diagram last set out above, at page 130, is, therefore, not accurate. The Court does not recognize a congressional power to move the dividing line between liberty and governmental authority. Yet Katzenbach v. Morgan has not been overruled, and it still stands as a possible authority if, at some time in the future, the Court again feels moved to recognize a substantive congressional power to define constitutional liberties. But an evaluation of the status of that case today must lead to the conclusion that it is no longer the law.

2. Liberty as a Protection from Private Intrusions

One other facet of the congressional implementation of constitutional liberty needs particular emphasis. Here we depart from our generalized analysis which defines constitutional liberty as opposition to governmental power. That definition is sound and accurate and extends to the wide range of constitutional liberties as we know them. There are exceptions, however, which must be considered.

The exceptions arise largely out of the Thirteenth Amendment, as mentioned in Chapter 2. The Thirteenth Amendment does not set individual constitutional liberty against exercises of governmental power. The Thirteenth Amendment prohibits slavery and involuntary servitude in the United States and constitutes a prohibition against either the government or a private citizen holding someone in slavery or involuntary servitude. This distinction between state or governmental action which is at the heart of the definition of most constitutional liberties and those few constitutional liberties which are not defined as in opposition to governmental power was discussed earlier in Chapter 2. Here this exceptional kind of constitutional liberty, a protection against intrusion by private persons, needs to be mentioned again in connection with congressional power to enforce liberty.

Until a few years ago, the Thirteenth Amendment had been effectively implemented only by legislation making it a crime for private citizens to hold other citizens in peonage. There had been a few convictions under those laws. In recent years, however, the Court has accepted the concept that *racial* discrimination is a "badge of slavery" within the meaning of the Thirteenth Amendment. In constitutional terms, private citizens engaging in racial discrimination can, therefore, violate the Constitution.

It is well to emphasize strongly that here we are talking only about *racial* discrimination. The other forms of discrimination in our society about which we have been concerned—religious discrimination, sex discrimination, discriminations based upon age and other aspects of status —are not protected from private actions within the scope of the Thirteenth Amendment. These other potential discriminations are still liberties which are protected only against governmental intrusion—the exercise of governmental power. The other substantive provisions of the Bill of Rights such as freedom of speech, freedom of religion, the protection of property rights, and the fundamental substantive due process rights such as the right to obtain birth control information and the right of pregnant women to have an abortion in the first trimester of pregnancy also are protected only against governmental intrusion.

There are two important recent cases which involve congressional legislation which, under the last section of the Thirteenth Amendment, protects private citizens against racial discrimination by other private citizens. The first of these is Jones v. Alfred H. Mayer Co., 392 U.S. 409 (1968), mentioned earlier at page 106. This case involved racial discrimination by the owner of realty refusing to sell the property to a black.

Suit was brought under 42 U.S.C.A. § 1982, a well-known statutory provision which was originally part of the civil rights legislation passed immediately at the end of the Civil War. This law provides:

> "All citizens of the United States shall have the same right, in every State and Territory, as is enjoyed by white citizens thereof to inherit, purchase, lease, sell, hold, and convey real and personal property."

This statutory provision had been a "dead letter" until the Jones v. Alfred Mayer case of 1968. In holding that this law prohibits private racial discrimination in the sale of property, the Court said:

> "We hold that § 1982 bars all racial discrimination, private as well as public, in the sale or rental of property, and that the statute, thus construed, is a valid exercise of the power of Congress to enforce the Thirteenth Amendment."

This decision is not analytically the same as the decision in Katzenbach v. Morgan, discussed at page 129, above, although it may appear to be. Rather, the Court was holding that the Constitution in the Thirteenth Amendment itself forbids racial discrimination as a "badge of slavery" by private citizens as well as by the government.

So all the congressional legislation does is simply implement the constitutional prohibition rather than create it.

The constitutional theory of this case was confirmed more recently in Runyon v. McCrary, 427 U.S. 160 (1976), mentioned earlier at page 106. This case involved the application of another aspect of the civil rights legislation passed immediately following the Civil War, in this instance, 42 U.S.C.A. § 1981. Relevant to this case is that portion of § 1981 which reads:

> "All persons within the jurisdiction of the United States shall have the same right in every State and Territory to make and enforce contracts, *   *   *."

Note that this statute is in a similar pattern to that of § 1982 involved in Jones v. Alfred Mayer.

The issue posed in Runyon v. McCrary is whether the refusal of a private school to admit a black student was in violation of the statute. The Court held "yes," on the ground that this was an interference with the right of the black parents to contract with the private school to have their child enter the school.

An interesting facet of this case is that four of the nine justices stated that Jones v. Alfred Mayer was incorrectly decided, not on constitutional but on statutory grounds. The assertion of these four justices was that the statute had been incorrectly applied. The framers of Sections 1981 and 1982 never intended that they were to be used to force citizens to make contracts with or sell property to people with whom they did not want to deal. But they do not deny the constitutional power of Congress under the Thirteenth Amendment to make such private racial discrimination the specific subject of civil or criminal liability.

These cases raise an important and critical question which is as yet unresolved. Do they mean that all racial discriminations by private citizens are unconstitutional unless such discriminations themselves are constitutionally protected? We know some such discriminations are constitutionally protected. As discussed before, the right to discriminate on a racial basis in the choice of a life partner, in the choice of friends, and in whom you invite into your home is almost certainly constitutionally protected as a substantive due process right of personal autonomy, or a "right to privacy" as the Court has rather ineptly called it. The right of the President to engage in racial discrimination in the selection of ambassadors and possibly also in the selection of cabinet members is constitutionally protected. But beyond these constitutional protections of permissible racial discrimination, is all racial discrimination now unconstitutional even though it emanates from private sources?

We cannot conclude this. Justice Powell in his concurring opinion in Runyon v. McCrary was careful to stress the narrowness of the holding as he saw it. He pointed out that this was a situation involving a private school which fulfilled the function of compulsory primary education and, thus, had a substantial public purpose. In addition, the majority opinion by Justice Stewart stressed that the Court was not deciding any question concerning the right of a private social organization to limit its membership on racial or any other grounds, the issue involved in Moose Lodge No. 107 v. Ervis, discussed at page 108.

Of far more critical importance analytically is the question whether this case changes the Court's earlier holdings which found no constitutional protection from racial discrimination by private businesses carried out against their employees or against customers. Those earlier holdings were based upon the state action requirement in the Fourteenth Amendment. Is this requirement now eliminated as far as racial discrimination is concerned? The constitutional issue is not being posed today because the provisions of the Civil Rights Act of 1964, passed under the federal power to regulate commerce, eliminate such discriminations generally, although some businesses are exempted from coverage.

It is clear from the majority and concurring opinions in Runyon v. McCrary that the Court is feeling its way on this issue. It does not yet appear ready to find all racial discrimination from private sources outlawed as a "badge of slavery" under the Thirteenth Amendment. Runyon v. McCrary and Jones v. Alfred Mayer can be narrowly applied in the future if the Court wishes to do so, but these decisions also open the door to a much broader application of the Thirteenth Amendment.

There are two other constitutional liberties of significance which the Court has found can be violated by private citizens. The first of these is the so-called "right to travel" or right to move from place to place within the United States. The Court has never related this right to any particular constitutional provision. It has simply recognized its existence and has stated that it is a right which goes beyond governmental action; it is a right which Congress can protect against intrusion by private citizens. The other major right of this kind is the right to participate in federal government activities, particularly federal elections, which the Congress can protect regardless of whether the intrusion is from a private source or a government source. Thus, Congress

can make it a crime to interfere with someone's
right to go to the polls to vote in a federal election, even though that interference is by a private citizen.

Finally, there is a closely related but more
complicated and little understood constitutional
protection of private rights. It is found in the
governmental power to protect from private intrusion the exercise of constitutional rights generally by private citizens. But the constitutional
rights here being protected are the traditional
liberties defined as protections from governmental intrusion. This special situation should not be
confused with the Thirteenth Amendment rights
discussed above.

Here examples are essential to understanding.
We are referring here to the right of the government to make it a crime for private citizens to interfere with school integration, for example. The
right to be free from discrimination in the public
schools is a traditional constitutional liberty as
defined against governmental power. But the
Congress can pass statutes protecting private citizens from the attempts of other private citizens
to interfere with the exercise of this public constitutional right defined as dependent upon state
action. Thus, Congress can make it an offense
for a private citizen to interfere with a black
going to an integrated school when the motive of

that private citizen is to interfere with the public constitutional right to attend public school without being discriminated against on the basis of race.

This principle has also been applied with respect to the use of other public facilities, such as public highways, public parks, and public buildings. Here it is established that Congress can pass legislation prohibiting private attempts to interfere with the use of these public facilities when the motive of the private citizen is to interfere with that public use. United States v. Guest, 383 U.S. 745 (1966). The significant factor in these cases is motive. If a private citizen blocks someone's use of the street with the motive of robbing him, there is no constitutional issue. But, if he blocks use of the street with the intention of stopping that use, this is a violation of the statute protecting the constitutional right to use the public street which in turn is based upon the constitutional right to use a public street without discrimination because the street has been supplied for use by all the public by the government.

3. Conclusion

This chapter explains the role of the legislative body in protecting the rights of the individual against the majority. In the past we have felt that legislative bodies, beholden to majorities, would not protect minorities' rights. This chapter reveals, however, that the protection of minorities by legislation has become a significant part of the protection of citizen liberties under our Constitution. The legislative role in protecting liberties is now established and firm.

CHAPTER 5

THE NATIONAL POWERS

1. National Powers and Liberty

Ours is a federal system. Through our Constitution we allocate the powers of government between the national government and the states. In the diagram thus far, the allocation of governmental powers had been presented in a simplistic sense. In this chapter, we shall develop and refine the diagram as it relates to the allocation of powers between the state and federal governments.

There are two basic considerations which must be stated and understood before an analysis of national powers is undertaken. First, implicit in all of the cases involving the scope of federal power and state power is the conclusion that the liberty-governmental power issue has already been resolved in favor of governmental power. If the attempt by the state or federal government to control private citizens falls within the area of liberty, then we need not concern ourselves with the allocation of power between the federal government and the states. In some of the cases involving the allocation of governmental power, the liberty question has been a serious one. But it was resolved before the issue of the allocation of power needed to be reached.

Second.   In internal governmental matters, it is elementary that the federal government is a government of delegated powers.   To justify an exercise of power by the national government, a specific provision or group of provisions must be found in the Constitution which authorize that exercise of federal power.   The states, on the other hand, have residual power—that is, all the powers not denied them by the Constitution.

To this second fundamental principle there is a caveat—a specific constitutional authorization for an exercise of federal power is needed only to carry out internal powers.   It has been established by Supreme Court decision that, in international affairs, the national government has inherent powers because in the world of nations, we must have status as a nation, with all a nation's powers.   The national government is, therefore, not limited to those powers which are delegated to it by the Constitution.   United States v. Curtiss-Wright Export Corp., 299 U.S. 304 (1936). Our federal system—the relationship between our states and the federal government—is an internal domestic matter.   It is not of concern to the nations of the world in their relations to us.

Both of these critical considerations are usefully demonstrated by using the Fair Labor Standards Act as an example. This is the federal law passed in 1938 which establishes minimum wages in the United States and provides that all hours worked over forty must be paid for by the employer at one and a half times the regular rate of pay (time-and-a-half). The statute also places limitations upon the use of child labor. The history of the constitutional litigation concerning this law demonstrates a liberty versus governmental power relationship. Comprehension of this relationship is essential to an understanding of the nature of constitutional cases once the Court gets into the issue of the allocation of power to the federal government or the states by the Constitution.

As late as 1936, the law of the Constitution as established by the Supreme Court was that minimum wage legislation, whether passed by the state governments or by the federal government and even limited to women and minors, was an unconstitutional intrusion upon individual liberty. Morehead v. People of State of New York ex rel. Tipaldo, 298 U.S. 587. If this holding had prevailed, the Fair Labor Standards Act would have been declared unconstitutional as a violation of individual liberty. The theory that this kind of social legislation violated the Constitution had been developed by the Court. It became known as the "freedom of contract" principle, although

the phrase "freedom of contract" appears no-
where in the Constitution. Under this theory,
general economic controls could be struck down
as constitutional violations on the ground that
they interfered with the right of individuals to
make whatever contracts they wanted to make.
This constitutional theory was broadened into an
"economic due process" principle. It was destroyed by the Court itself shortly after the *Tipaldo* decision in the case upholding the constitutionality of the Fair Labor Standards Act, United
States v. Darby Lumber Co., 312 U.S. 100 (1941).

As late as 1935, in Schechter Poultry Corp. v.
United States, 295 U.S. 495, the Supreme Court
had held that the federal power to regulate interstate commerce did not extend to the economic
regulation of wages and prices of a wholesaler
who received goods from outside the state and
sold them wholly within the state. Following
this precedent, it could have been concluded that
unconstitutionality was even clearer in the attempt to control prices and wages of a retailer
selling wholly within the state. Again, if this
holding had persisted, the Supreme Court would
have held the Fair Labor Standards Act unconstitutional on the ground that the regulation did not
fall within federal power because the statute,
which did apply to wholesalers who received
goods from interstate commerce but sold them

only in the state, was also later to be applied to retailers.

This earlier line of authority also was reversed by the Supreme Court in the case of United States v. Darby Lumber Co., mentioned above. This is the case which upheld the constitutionality of the Fair Labor Standards Act, both against a liberty challenge that a control of minimum wages violated the liberty of the workers who wished to work for less than the minimum wage and against a lack of federal power challenge that businesses wholly within the state but which received goods from outside the state were not subject to federal control under the commerce power.

The usefulness of this brief exercise in analysis is to demonstrate that the liberty issue is always present in a case involving the allocation of powers between the federal and state governments. Sometimes the liberty issue is a serious one, as the discussion of three later important cases will show.

In terms of our diagram, analysis of the *Darby* case reveals that the issue of the constitutionality of the Fair Labor Standards Act was raised both with respect to the liberty issue where the numeral ① appears, and with respect to the issue of federal power where the numeral ② appears. Even if the Court had held that there was no constitutional liberty to be protected, the Court, if it had followed prior authority, would have held that such wage and hour control was not within the province of the federal government but within the province only of the states. The Court, nevertheless, held that the case fell within the area of federal power. Hence, the asterisk, representing the decision, appearing immediately beside the numeral ② in the federal power division of our diagram:

2. The Sweep of Federal Commerce Power

This preliminary analysis has set the stage for the analysis of the federal powers under the Constitution. The Constitution is read to give a broad scope to the powers of the national government delegated by it to the national government. These powers are found largely in Article I, Section 8. The Great Chief Justice, John Marshall, established the pattern for broad interpretation in two famous cases during his unparalleled leadership on the Court.

In 1819, in McCulloch v. Maryland, 17 U.S. (4 Wheat.) 316, Chief Justice Marshall, speaking for the unanimous Court, upheld the power of the federal government to create a United States bank, although there is no specific reference to the power to create a bank in the Constitution itself.

The Court reasoned that the creation of a bank was the establishment of an instrumentality of government to aid in carrying out other powers granted to the federal government such as the power to coin money and regulate currency, the power to tax and spend money, the power to regulate interstate commerce, the power to raise and support the military forces, and so on. Specifically, the source of this federal power was seen as enamating from the "necessary and proper" clause which concludes Article I, Section 8. The Court saw this clause not as a limitation upon the power of the federal government, but as an additional grant of power. And in a classic exposition of constitutional interpretation, Marshall in his opinion established that the word "necessary" really means "appropriate." A U. S. bank is an "appropriate" means of governmental control. Yet it certainly is not "necessary" in any strict sense—we have been without one since 1836!

The impact of this decision was to establish a pattern of broad and nonobstructive interpretation of the delegated federal power as a means of undergirding a strong national government.

Five years later, again speaking for a unanimous Court, Chief Justice Marshall was faced with the interpretation and application of the clause in Article I, Section 8, giving the federal government power to regulate interstate and foreign commerce. This is the clause upon which today most of the federal internal governmental regulations are based. The case is Gibbons v. Ogden, 22 U.S. (9 Wheat.) 1 (1824). The purport of the opinion in this case was that any activity that "affects" matters beyond state lines is within the federal power to control. The definition of the scope of federal power given in that case is still the "test" used in such cases, insofar as complicated constitutional matters can be made subject to a test. The phrase the Court still uses to define the breadth of the federal power under the commerce clause is: "affecting interstate commerce."

Three modern cases, in addition to United States v. Darby, set out above, define today's breadth of national power stemming from the commerce clause. The first of these is National Labor Relations Board v. Jones and Laughlin Steel Corp., 301 U.S. 1 (1937). This is the case which ended an era approximating the first third of this century under which the Court had fallen into the pattern of giving a restrictive interpretation to federal power over interstate commerce rather than the broad interpretation which had been the theme from the days of John Marshall. This case, concluding that era, upheld the constitutionality of the National Labor Relations Act, as it applied to large but also to small predominantly intrastate businesses. It was recognized in its time as a landmark case because the National Labor Relations Act provided for the coverage of all businesses which "affect" commerce, and the Court upheld this definition (or this "test," if you will) as being constitutionally acceptable.

Of much more critical importance in defining the scope of federal power precisely is the case of Wickard v. Filburn, 317 U.S. 111 (1942). The facts of this case are important to an understanding of its constitutional impact. Filburn owned and operated quite a small farm in Montgomery County, Ohio. It had been his practice to raise a small acreage of winter wheat and to sell a portion of it, to feed a portion to his poultry and livestock, to use some in making flour for home consumption, and to keep the rest for seeding. Under the Federal Agricultural Adjustment Act of 1938, he was awarded a wheat acreage allotment of 11.1 acres. The statute provided that if he planted in excess of this amount he would be assessed a penalty of 49¢ a bushel. Instead of limiting his wheat production to 11.1 acres, he sowed and harvested 23 acres. He refused to pay the assessed penalty of $117.11. The critical fact in this case is that Filburn planned to sell none of his wheat that year. He had grown the entire 23 acres for his own consumption on his own farm.

Here our dual constitutional analysis comes into play. There is a genuine liberty question whether either government, state or federal, can control the amount of wheat a farmer can grow on his own property for his own use. The Court's answer to this issue was that Mr. Filburn's "right" to grow a certain amount of wheat on his own farm for his own use did not fall in the area of an individual liberty. For purposes of regulating the overall national production of wheat, government can control the amount of wheat a particular farmer grows, even for his own use.

The validity of this principle can be seen if we merely substitute opium poppies for wheat. There is no constitutional liberty to grow opium poppies for your own use. So we can control what you produce in your own home for your own use. Consider as a more complete analogy the matter of home sewing. When this nation is at war and we are rationing the purchase of clothes, we would have to control the clothes made by persons in their own homes to make that rationing effective. Otherwise, the rationing system would break down and the use of cloth would not be curtailed. So the Court concludes that there was governmental power to ration the growing of wheat, even though that wheat was grown totally for home consumption. Thus, Mr. Filburn's liberty contention failed.

But then the question arose: Did the national government have the power to reach so deeply into local affairs that it could direct a farmer not to grow 11.9 additional acres of wheat. Even granting that a state government could do this, which would show that there was no liberty issue, does the federal power to regulate interstate commerce reach so deeply into the local life of citizens that it could control this wheat production for personal use?

The Court's answer was to uphold the federal power to regulate. In a careful and effective opinion by Justice Jackson, the Court conceded that such a small quantity of locally grown wheat considered separately obviously had no substantial national effect upon commerce. But the cumulative effect of many small farmers refusing to follow the wheat allocation could have a most serious effect upon the interstate and international market in wheat. As the Court said: "Such wheat overhangs the market." If the prices go up, the wheat, supposedly grown for home consumption, will tend to flow into the market and create the problem of surplus again.

With such a broad holding, however, where is the limit? If the federal government can reach into the small home and the small farm, have we not defined the scope of federal power so broadly that it extends to virtually all possible governmental regulation? The case of Wickard v. Filburn properly raises the question of whether our diagram on a quantitative basis should look like this:

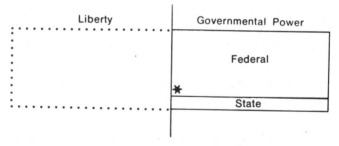

Note: The location of the asterisk shows the case of Wickard v. Filburn, close to the liberty line and extending federal power deeply into local matters.

[B7220]

We must recognize, however, that there is overlap between state and federal powers so that the great breadth of federal power does not automatically mean that state power is reduced virtually to nothingness.

From this analysis of the case of Wickard v. Filburn, we can develop a simple question to help resolve possible confusion of the "liberty" issue with the "scope of federal power" issue. Assume that Congress passes a statute requiring all motorcyclists and bicycle riders to wear hard helmets. Assume you are doubtful about the constitutionality of such a statute. Ask yourself this question: Could a state or local government pass such a statute? If your answer is: "No, I don't think a state or a city could," your concern is with liberty. If your answer is: "Oh, yes, a state or city could," then you have no liberty question; your real concern is only the distribution of power between the state and federal governments.

Or take a reverse situation where a state simply outlaws all two-wheeled motor vehicles on public highways. It applies this law so that motorcyclists cannot even drive into the state from other states. If you doubt the constitutionality of this law, as well you might, ask yourself this question: "Could Congress outlaw all motorcycles on public highways?" If your answer is: "No," then you are thinking in terms of liberty. You are asserting that constitutional liberty forbids either the federal government or the states from outlawing all motorcycles on public highways. But if your answer is: "Yes, Congress could do it," then you are thinking in terms of

[*157*]

the distribution of power between state and federal governments. You are asserting that the state is placing a burden on interstate transportation and that this violates the distribution of powers between the state and federal governments, but that the federal government could pass this law under the power to regulate interstate commerce.

The purpose of this exercise with these two hypothetical situations is to aid in the analysis of any case when it contains both substantial liberty and distribution of governmental power issues, as did the case of Wickard v. Filburn. By asking whether *the other* government could engage in this regulation, you are isolating the liberty question from the distribution of governmental powers question. In class with Constitutional Law students, I have found the use of this question valuable in enabling students to see the essential nature of their own constitutional doubts with respect to a particular statute.

The third recent and critically important Supreme Court case defining the scope of federal power under the commerce clause also fulfills an additional purpose. In it we see the use of governmental legislation to protect personal liberty, but not constitutionally preserved liberty. Katzenbach v. McClung, 379 U.S. 294 (1964).

The comprehensive Civil Rights Act of 1964 prohibits discrimination based upon race, religion, national origin, and sex. Both discrimination in hiring employees and in serving customers is prohibited. The businesses covered by the statute include hotels and motels, restaurants, and industrial enterprises of any substantial size.

A companion case decided the same day as the case here discussed should be mentioned briefly. In it the Court held that a motel in downtown Atlanta which served interstate travelers was forbidden to discriminate on a racial basis and that this discrimination could be prohibited within the constitutional power of the federal government. Heart of Atlanta Motel v. United States, 379 U.S. 241 (1964). There is little difficulty with this holding. The burdens upon interstate commerce of the inability of racial minorities to obtain accommodations while traveling from state to state is manifest.

While there was a claim made concerning the liberty of the motel operator to discriminate on a racial basis, this constitutional challenge also easily failed. There has been a tradition since the ancient common law that the innkeeper was obligated to take all travelers of proper deportment and with adequate funds without any discrimination. It would be a reversal of centuries of learning suddenly to have found that there was a con-

stitutional right in a public innkeeper to discriminate on a racial basis.

The far more critical case was the suit by Mc-
Clung against Attorney General Katzenbach to
test the constitutionality of the Civil Rights Act
in prohibiting discrimination against customers
in the case of McClung's restaurant, known as Ollie's Barbecue, in Birmingham, Alabama.

Ollie's Barbecue discriminated against black
customers as a regular policy. There was, however, no showing that the restaurant ever had
served or was likely to serve any interstate cus-
tomer. The Civil Rights Act—Section 201 (b) (2)
and (c)—provides, however, that a restaurant is
covered if "*   *   * a substantial portion of the
food which it serves   *   *   * has moved in
commerce." The facts showed that 46% of the
food served in the restaurant while purchased
locally had its origin outside the state. There
was, therefore, no question about statutory coverage. The only issue was whether the federal constitutional power to control interstate commerce
could reach so far. The Court held that it could,
upholding the right of black persons to be served
without discrimination at Ollie's Barbecue.

The troublesome aspect of this case lies in the
fact that there is no showing that racial discrimination in this and other similar local restaurants
would actually affect interstate commerce just

because some of the food served at the restaurant came originally from outside the state. The people of Birmingham, Alabama, had to eat. If black people were not able to eat at Ollie's Barbecue, they were going to eat somewhere else, and the consumption of food from outside the state would remain about the same. At least there was no showing in the case that there would be any reduction in the food imported into Alabama from other states if racial discrimination continued in restaurants in Alabama.

Because of this troublesome difficulty in relating the racial discrimination at Ollie's Barbecue to an effect upon interstate commerce, Justice Black in a concurring opinion said that whether or not interstate commerce was cut down, it was "distorted." He never defined what this distortion was, and this was an entirely new concept never before referred to or relied upon in cases.

The majority opinion also was unsatisfactory. There was a general discussion of the fact that blacks probably eat out less because of the discrimination, and there was general emphasis upon the probable inhibitions on interstate travel by blacks because of difficulty in finding accommodations. But these factors were not directly related to a restaurant which had never been known to serve an interstate traveler, regardless of race. Of at least some substance in the majority opinion was the claim that such discrimination probably deters professional and skilled people from moving into areas where discrimination is prevalent, causing industry to be reluctant to locate there. This statement was made, and would have some impact, except there was no real indication of supporting evidence in the record.

The majority opinion did conclude, however, that all of these factors taken together probably caused some fewer sales of food in restaurants than would otherwise have been sold in public eating places. The only trouble with this conclusion is that it still does not establish that fewer sales in restaurants would in any way cut down on the total amount of food shipped in interstate commerce into Alabama, a fact which would seem to be requisite to the showing of an interstate effect.

The decision is correct, but the opinions are not adequate. The Court was too timid in not writing broadly enough to justify its decision on clear and established constitutional grounds. Cases like Wickard v. Filburn demonstrate that purely local production and consumption of wheat has an effect upon the interstate market. It should appear from the Wickard v. Filburn analysis that Congress could constitutionally control the discriminatory practices of every public eating place in the United States.

Many public eating places serve interstate travelers. Under the reasoning of the motel case, there is no question that Congress can regulate those restaurants. Then, the next logical step is clear. Restaurants which serve interstate customers and therefore by federal law can be forbidden to discriminate on a racial basis are placed at an economic disadvantage in competition with restaurants that do not serve interstate customers and do discriminate on a racial basis. So Congress, if it wants to, can correct that local discriminatory impact by protecting the economic foundation of the restaurants which serve interstate customers and are not discriminating. Congress can be seen as taking the position that to insure adequate facilities available for interstate commerce on a nondiscriminatory basis, all restaurants, whether they serve interstate customers or not, can be controlled. Otherwise the local restaurants not serving interstate customers and discriminating in accordance with local prejudices would place the interstate restaurants at a serious competitive disadvantage. This in turn would make compliance with the law of Congress difficult, and Congress can protect against the onslaught of any local practices which interfere with its valid regulatory schemes. Congress did exactly this in rationing homegrown wheat production because of its effect on the interstate market.

Once it is established that Congress could constitutionally eliminate discriminations based upon race, religion, sex, and national origin with respect to customers in all restaurants in the United States, then there is no longer any serious constitutional problem in enacting a statute which covers only some restaurants—only those restaurants which serve interstate customers plus those, such as Ollie's Barbecue, which import in interstate commerce a substantial portion of the food which they serve.

Under this rationale, it is not the effect upon commerce created by the purchase of the food across state lines which justifies the constitutional reach of the federal government to control the restaurant. It is the constitutional right of Congress to control the entire restaurant market to protect those restaurants whose activities do affect interstate commerce.

The recent cases, particularly Wickard v. Filburn and Katzenbach v. McClung, unquestionably give a broad sweep to the general power of the federal government to control small local activities. Even without including the broad sweep of other federal powers listed in Article I, Section 8, current federal power reaches far into local affairs under the power to regulate commerce.

3. Is Federal Power All-Inclusive?

The question posed in connection with the discussion of Wickard v. Filburn needs reiteration. Is there anything left to the states? Even assuming that the states have power to regulate if the federal government has not undertaken to do so (a topic which will be discussed in the next chapter) has the federal power now been extended to virtually all aspects of our lives through the broad interpretations of the commerce power and through the other powers of the federal government? In our diagram, does the federal power cover the entire area of potential governmental power or leave only the narrowest sliver of exclusive state power, as postulated above at page 156? If this is the current state of the development then our federal system is a far different system than it was when it was created. Do we still have a federal system or is all governmental power lodged in the national government? Do the states continue to play a role only at the sufferance of the federal government?

There are even more extreme examples of the reach of federal power than those which have been the subject of decisions in the United States Supreme Court. One such example is the 1974 amendment to the Fair Labor Standards Act which requires the payment of the national minimum wage to domestic employees in private homes throughout the United States. In passing statutes under the commerce power, Congress usually puts in a preamble a description of the effect upon interstate commerce of the activity which it is undertaking to control. Congress did this in its preamble to the Civil Rights Act of 1964. But in the passage of this amendment to the Fair Labor Standards Act to require that the minimum wage be paid domestic servants, the Congress did not even attempt to use any words to relate the coverage of this statute to the federal power over interstate commerce. But no case has made a constitutional challenge of this law as being beyond federal power, although this statute reaches deeply into local matters.

Yet, the Court should be expected to uphold its constitutionality. The payment of less than the minimum wage to domestic servants has the same kind of cumulative impact on the economy of the nation that the cumulative impact of small farmers growing wheat in excess of quota, even for use on their own farms, would have. There is no impact on interstate commerce in the failure of one homeowner to pay less than the minimum wage to one domestic servant. But when several hundred thousand of such instances are added together, there will be a significant economic impact upon the nation. And this economic impact would be adequate support for a constitutional holding authorizing the federal legislation.

So again let us inquire, is there anything left not within the federal commerce power? It may be difficult to pick out particular situations that would not be within federal power, and those who teach and write in this area are reluctant to give such examples. But there is another side to this analysis, and it is an important one: Most of the law which controls the lives of American citizens even today is state and local law. It has become customary in recent years to talk of the long reach of federal power or the tentacles of federal power. So this fact bears repeating and emphasis: Most of the law which controls our lives still is state and local law.

The criminal law that protects the lives and property of citizens from assaults and thefts by other citizens is state law. The law controlling the buying and selling of property is state law. The law concerning commercial transactions is state contract law. The laws concerning automobile accidents is state tort law. The entire field of family law and domestic relations is state law. The most important single governmental function after the protection of the citizen's life and property is undoubtedly education. The schools are set up under state and local law. We have local zoning of property and local control of highway and street construction and use.

There is little federal intrusion into this great mass of state and local law that controls our lives. If there is intrusion, it is justified constitutionally on a narrow and specific ground such as the elimination of racial or sex discrimination, or it is concerned with the regulation of certain businesses which have obvious interstate impact such as transportation, television, and industrial production. It may be difficult to define how deeply Congress could constitutionally intrude in these broad areas of state and local law, but the realistic fact is that Congress is not doing so and there is no indication that it will do so. So we need not assume that our diagram must show a modern federal sweep of power that covers all governmental power.

As a summary of our situation with respect to federal power today, while remembering that the states also exercise much of the power in the federal area, as the next chapter shows, perhaps we should draw our diagram about like this:

```
                    |
       Liberty      |      Governmental Power
· · · · · · · · · · |· · · · _____
·                   |      |
·                   |      |
·                   |      |         Federal
·                   |      |
·                   |      |_____
·                   |      |
·                   |      |          State
· · · · · · · · · · |· · · |_____
                    |                    [B7219]
                    |
```

4. The Power to Tax and Spend for the General Welfare

The first listed power delegated to Congress in Article I, Section 8, of the Constitution affords us a productive opportunity for constitutional analysis. The federal power to tax and spend for the general welfare fell victim to a clearly illogical analysis by the Supreme Court.

Until the year 1936, we had had no authoritative adjudication resolving a major constitutional ambiguity: Does the phrase "general welfare" in the granting of taxing and spending powers to the federal government constitute simply a summary of the other powers granted immediately following in the same section, or does it constitute an additional grant of power. If Congress was authorized to tax and spend money for a "general welfare" which goes beyond the other delegated powers, this would mean that Congress could *spend* money in connection with subjects

[*169*]

which otherwise are not within the scope of federal *regulatory* power.

A particular application of this issue would be to ask if Congress could spend money for a subject which was not within the federal power to control interstate commerce. Could Congress spend money for maternity welfare in the various states even under the assumption that there was no general regulatory power, under the commerce clause or otherwise, enabling the federal government to deal with maternity welfare problems? Cf. Massachusetts v. Mellon, 262 U.S. 447 (1923).

This dispute over the meaning of the Constitution was resolved by a holding of the Supreme Court in the case involving the constitutionality of the Agricultural Adjustment Act of 1933. United States v. Butler, 297 U.S. 1 (1936). The statute set up a scheme for the payment of benefits to farmers in return for their promises to restrict part of their agricultural production. The Court considered the more restrictive theory that "general welfare" simply summarizes the other delegated powers, but then specifically adopted the broader theory that the power of Congress to tax and spend for the "general welfare" constitutes a grant of an additional power beyond the other powers given to Congress in Article I, Section 8, of the Constitution.

[*170*]

In terms of our diagram, this holding means that the power to tax and spend for the general welfare expands the area of federal power. The dotted line symbolically shows the scope of federal power before this decision adopting the broader application of the "general welfare" clause, and the solid line indicates the extent of federal power after the adoption of this constitutional interpretation in 1936. The area contained between the dotted line and the solid line is the additional breadth of federal power created by the Court's interpretation that Congress can tax and spend concerning subject matter it otherwise does not have the power to regulate:

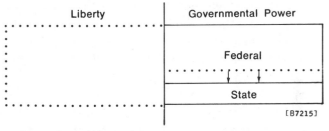

The next step in constitutional analysis in the case, then, should have been a determination of whether making payments to farmers to restrict production was "for the general welfare." The obvious purpose of this analysis would be to see whether Congress had the power to spend money for this purpose, since its spending can only be for the general welfare. (All this was under the assumption that Congress did not have the power to regulate agricultural production. The holding recognizing Congress' power to regulate agricultural production came later in the case of Wickard v. Filburn, discussed at page 153.)

Instead of taking the next logical step, these startling words appear in Justice Roberts' opinion for the Court immediately after he adopts the broad view that Congress may tax and spend for the general welfare beyond its regulatory powers:

> "We are not now required to ascertain the scope of the phrase 'general welfare of the United States' or to determine whether an appropriation in aid of agriculture falls within it. Wholly apart from that question, another principle imbedded in our Constitution prohibits the enforcement of the Agricultural Adjustment Act. The act invades the reserved rights of the states. * * *" 297 U.S. at 68.

The total failure of this analysis should be clear. If the case falls within the power delegated to Congress to tax and spend for the general welfare, it cannot "invade the reserved rights of the states." Our diagram shows this. In effect, what the Court did was say that the federal power did extend to the solid dividing line in the diagram, set out above, but that actually in doing so, it extended beyond the dotted line and therefore intruded upon state power.

So what the Court did in this case was to say it did not have to decide whether the spending fell within federal power because the spending invaded the reserved rights of the states. There is, of course, no such constitutional doctrine, nor can there be, under the supremacy clause of the Constitution.

In deference to an attempt to understand the Court's opinion in this case, it should be stated that immediately following the quotation set out above, the Court did refer to an assertion that this spending for the general welfare was a "regulation" of agricultural production. Then in a rather confused way, the opinion tried to demonstrate that the program, by setting up conditions for the receipt of the funds, went beyond the virtually universal device of controlling the way money granted under the general welfare clause is spent.

The Court actually was unable to establish this as a regulation rather than a taxing and spending scheme because conditional grants of the money, as Justice Stone so ably pointed out in his dissenting opinion, had been upheld over and over again by the Supreme Court. And what was involved in this case was a system of conditional grants of money. Further, if the Court really

[*173*]

felt that this was regulation in the guise of taxing and spending, it was improper to treat it as a taxing and spending case and to make the constitutional holding that the taxing and spending power was an additional grant of power to Congress.

There really is no escape from the conclusion that the Court in this case failed to follow elementary constitutional analysis, as is demonstrated in the diagram, that the exercise of a delegated constitutional power by Congress cannot invade the powers of the states. As a reminder, it should be said again that an attempt to exercise a delegated power must be tested as to whether it is an invasion of liberty, and that question is an important and difficult one. But if it is an exercise of federal delegated power, then it cannot invade the powers of the states.

Without specifically overruling United States v. Butler, the Court the next year upheld in Helvering v. Davis, 301 U.S. 619 (1937), the constitutionality of the Social Security old age benefits paid directly by the federal government. In this case, the Court made the specific finding that providing old age pensions was a matter of the "general welfare" of the United States.

Every cent which the federal government spends is subject to finding constitutional authorization to spend. This spending must be either

[*174*]

on behalf of one of the specific powers delegated to the federal government, or must be for the "general welfare." There are a number of well-known instances where the federal government spends money in ways which do not appear to fall within the general regulatory powers of the federal government and must be accepted as spending authorized solely by the general welfare clause. The federal government issues and sells or gives away many pamphlets on such diverse topics as dressmaking in the home, how best to occupy leisure time, beaver-raising, home canning, and the list goes on and on. The expenditure of the funds to publish these pamphlets must be attributable to the federal power to spend for the general welfare.

Much more obvious and important examples are federal aid to education, federal aid to housing, and other similar programs which so far have never been considered to fall within the federal power over interstate and foreign commerce or other delegated powers to regulate. These important federal spending programs carry with them limitations and conditions upon the expenditure of the money. These are the same kinds of limitations and conditions which were contained in the Agricultural Adjustment Act and which were found to be "regulatory" in United States v. Butler. *Butler* must simply be put down as one of the stark examples of faulty constitutional analysis within the Supreme Court itself.

5. The Treaty Power and the Liberty-Governmental Power Analysis

A few years ago in the United States, we had a major political and constitutional controversy over the federal power to make treaties. This controversy arose because of the failure of many lawmakers to understand the basic analysis presented in this book. The lawmakers failed to separate the liberty issue from the federal/state governmental power issue.

This controversy over the treaty-making power affords a useful summary of this chapter which has as its theme the interrelationship between constitutional liberty and federal and state powers.

The origins of the controversy are found in the case of Missouri v. Holland, 252 U.S. 416 (1920). Congress had undertaken the protection of migratory birds by passing a statute applicable throughout the United States. Lower federal courts had held this statute unconstitutional on the ground that it was beyond the federal power to regulate interstate commerce. The United States then concluded a treaty with Canada concerning the protection of migratory birds. Congress passed a statute to implement this treaty which had the same impact on the local control of migratory birds that the earlier statute had.

The Supreme Court, in a famous opinion by Justice Holmes, held that regardless of whether the congressional statute passed prior to the treaty was within congressional power, the congressional statute to protect migratory birds in the United States was clearly within federal power once the treaty with Canada had been concluded. Thus, the treaty had authorized what amounted to an increase in federal power.

Justice Holmes' opinion was cryptic. It is rather difficult to find out exactly what his analysis was meant to convey except that it was obvious he had a great love for migratory birds. He did point out that the Constitution provides that acts of Congress have to be made "in pursuance of the Constitution" but treaties, in the actual wording of Article VI, Clause 2, need be made only "under the authority of the United States." He said that he did not mean to imply that there were no limitations on the treaty-making power, but, he said in his opinion, "They must be ascertained in a different way." But then he did not tell us what that way was.

This case, absent careful analysis of its nature, could leave someone with the feeling that Congress can create power by making treaties in ways which could be detrimental to the liberties

[*177*]

of American citizens. The possibility that Congress might, for example, be able to inhibit the free speech of American citizens by signing a treaty began to concern a number of people. Suppose that the United States and the Soviet Union concluded a treaty under which each promised to suppress criticism of the government of the other nation. This kind of treaty obviously would run afoul of the constitutional liberty of free speech in the United States unless there is some magic in the treaty-making power which would enable an intrusion upon constitutional liberties by treaty.

In any event, the controversy over the so-called Bricker Amendment began. Senator Bricker proposed, and in 1953 the Senate Judiciary Committee recommended, a constitutional amendment which provided as its two essential elements:

> (1) A provision of a treaty which conflicts with any provision of this Constitution shall not be of any force or effect;
>
> (2) A treaty shall become effective as internal law in the United States only through legislation by Congress which it could enact under its delegated powers in the absence of such treaty.

After several years of heated controversy, which produced voluminous discussion, this attempt to propose a constitutional amendment never succeeded.

The argument on behalf of the Bricker Amendment was that Congress and the President by the "bootstrap" device of making a treaty could increase their own powers. If the constitutional principle actually had been that Congress could stop Americans from criticizing Russia by concluding a treaty with Russia, the proponents of the amendment would have had a compelling case. Such, however, was not legally sound. We know this is so if we follow the analysis presented in this book.

There is no question that Missouri v. Holland is correct in holding that a treaty with a foreign country can increase the delegated powers of the federal government *as against state power*. The first treaty ever concluded by the federal government in its history did exactly that. The most common treaty which the United States government makes is a commercial treaty with a foreign nation. These treaties authorize our citizens to go into other countries and carry on business and trade, own property, and use the courts on a reciprocal basis just as our nation is giving similar rights to the citizens of the other nations. We have concluded hundreds of these treaties; no one has ever doubted their constitutionality. Yet the Bricker Amendment would have destroyed them all. In implementing those treaties on a domestic level, Congress passes legislation which compels state and local governments to recognize the rights of aliens. Without such treaties, Congress has been assumed not to have this power.

The matter of ownership of property, the right to go into business and to obtain local licenses to go into business, and the right to use the local courts are all matters which we have assumed are not within the federal power. These are local matters for state and local legislation. Yet from the very beginning, the national government has made these reciprocal commercial treaties which forced local acceptance of commercial activities by foreigners. So it is true that Missouri v. Holland is good law. The treaty involved in that case gave the federal government the power to regulate (as against state power) in a field where we can assume that Congress had no power to regulate in the absence of the treaty, at least at that time.

Look at our diagram. What Missouri v. Holland held was that federal power can be expanded within the constitutional area of governmental power by the conclusion of a valid treaty with a foreign nation. And this is what the commercial treaties do. Thus, the line drawn between federal and state power is moved down, federal power is expanded from the dotted line to the solid line:

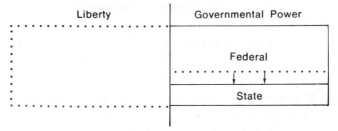

Effect of treaty-making power on federal power. Note it has no impact on liberty.

[B7223]

What is absolutely critical to the analysis and what the proponents of the Bricker Amendment never understood is that these commercial treaties and the Missouri v. Holland treaty never in the slightest degree sanctioned the expansion of governmental power as against constitutional liberty—the moving of the basic dividing line between governmental power and liberty to the left to cut down on constitutional liberty and to expand governmental power.

The two constitutional issues are totally different. There has never been a hint in any Supreme Court case that a treaty could sanction a congressional intrusion upon liberty. The proposal of the Bricker Amendment stemmed from the failure to understand that the expansion of federal power in the area of admitted governmental power is a wholly different thing under our Constitu-

[*181*]

tion from the expansion of governmental power in the area of liberty.

The amendment would have been an unwise and tragic limitation upon our power as a nation in the family of nations. If it had passed, our commercial treaties and commercial interchanges with other nations would have been made exceedingly difficult, and we would not have achieved any additional protection in the area that the proponents of the amendment said was so important—individual liberty. Cooler heads and sounder analysis ultimately prevailed so the Senate did not garner the requisite two-thirds vote to propose the amendment for adoption. Individual liberty was never threatened and never yet has been threatened by the treaty-making power of the federal government.

6. Conclusion

We complete our discussion of the breadth of federal power under the Constitution with a notation that the other powers in Article I, Section 8, have been given broad interpretations comparable to the federal power to regulate commerce and to tax and spend. The powers of the national government are sweeping, but, as has been pointed out above, most of the law which organizes our society and controls our lives is, nevertheless, still state and local law.

CHAPTER 6

STATE POWERS

1. The Implied Constitutional Prohibition Against State Power over Interstate Commerce

During the first half of the nineteenth century, the Supreme Court was particularly troubled by the issue of whether the delegation of powers to the national government under Article I, Section 8, of the Constitution constituted an implied denial of the same powers to the states. As to some of the powers it appeared rather certain that the nature of the power delegated did constitute a denial of similar power to the states. In the case of the power to exercise exclusive legislation over the District of Columbia, the denial of state power is obvious. This implied denial of state power, which came to be known as the "implied prohibition" upon state power, was assumed to apply to the federal war power, the postal power, the power to coin money, and the power to provide for and regulate bankruptcy. Further, it was early held that the power of the federal government to control admiralty and maritime matters was an exclusive power. Strangely enough, this power was implied in the federal government from Article III, Section 2, the judiciary article of the Constitution, and its reference to "admiralty and maritime Jurisdiction," coupled with the circumstance that much maritime jurisdiction is international.

Yet, on the other hand, it was just as clear from the beginning that the delegation of power to the Congress to lay and collect taxes did not constitute an implied prohibition against the states' power to levy taxes. The delegated power to borrow money on the credit of the United States was not a denial of the power in the states to borrow money on the credit of the states.

The critical and often litigated issue concerning an implied prohibition against state power to regulate where there admittedly is federal power arose under the grant of power to regulate interstate and foreign commerce. The great early leading case was Gibbons v. Ogden, 22 U.S. (9 Wheat.) 1 (1824), mentioned in Chapter 5. That case involved the enforcement by the state of New York of a monopoly license for steamships as it applied to ferries crossing the Hudson River from New York to New Jersey and back. The New York courts had held that the exclusive license given to Robert Fulton and others forbade a New Jersey-owned steampowered ferry from crossing the Hudson River into New York.

Chief Justice Marshall's pioneering opinion under the commerce clause held that the federal

power over commerce did not stop at the state
lines. It included the power to preserve interstate commerce as it penetrated into the states.
In his far-reaching discussion, Marshall considered whether any power to regulate interstate
commerce remained in the states. He came to
the very brink of accepting Daniel Webster's
strong argument that the delegation to the federal government of power over interstate commerce
required a uniform regulation throughout the
United States which would deny the power to
regulate in the states. Certainly constitutional
experts at that time seemed to accept this view.
But as Chief Justice Marshall neared the end of
his opinion, and while recognizing "great force in
this argument," he turned away from it and
found simply that the state regulation interfered
with the federal coast-wide shipping license
which the New Jersey ferry owner had. This
finding meant that there was a conflict between
state and federal law. When there is such a conflict, federal law prevails under Article VII, second clause, the "supremacy" clause.

Chief Justice Marshall's prescient wisdom was
demonstrated by his unwillingness to accept a full
prohibition against state power in regulating interstate commerce. Five years later Marshall
wrote for the Court in Willson v. Black Bird
Creek Marsh Co., 27 U.S. (2 Pet.) 245 (1829).

This case involved a Delaware legislative authorization for the building of a dam across a local navigable creek. Because the creek was navigable, there was no question that the federal government had power to control the uses of the creek and the building of a dam across it. But Congress had not engaged in any such regulation. Marshall for the Court found that the authorization of the dam by the state could not be considered "as repugnant to the power to regulate commerce in its dormant state." This holding was the first recognition by the Supreme Court that the grant of federal power over commerce did not constitute a complete implied prohibition against the states regulating interstate commerce.

The matter continued to be troublesome, however, and some justices of the Court continued to take the flat position that there was no state power to regulate interstate commerce at all. It was recognized that the commerce clause itself did constitute an implied prohibition against the states regulating in some ways in the interstate commerce field, but the *Black Bird Creek Marsh Co.* case recognized that the states would be allowed to regulate in other ways.

The reconciling of these two viewpoints took place in the 1851 case of Cooley v. Board of Wardens of the Port of Philadelphia, 53 U.S. (12 How.) 299. Justice Curtis, writing for the Court, but not without dissent, established the distinction between those matters involving commerce in which the states continue to have constitutional power to regulate and those matters in which the Constitution itself forbids the state exercise of power.

The Court's distinction was to treat differently "national" interstate commerce and "local" interstate commerce. As to national matters, the states have no power in the commerce field, but as to local matters, they do have power. The justification for the distinction was found to lie in the need for some interstate commerce always to be regulated on a uniform basis. These matters require the exclusive legislation by Congress. But other aspects of interstate commerce allow diversity to meet local needs. These are the local areas that permit state control. This distinction has prevailed effectively to the present time, although obviously refined and adjusted to take care of modern developments.

To represent this in our diagram, we now divide the federal power and show an overlapping of federal and state powers. We continue to use a solid line for the federal powers, and we use a jagged line to show the extent of the state powers. Our diagram appears this way, as it represents the nature of the power to regulate interstate commerce:

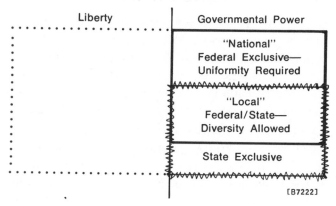

[B7222]

In the middle area of the diagram where federal and state power overlap, note that diversity is "allowed." There never was any doubt in the *Cooley* case that, if the federal government wished to undertake regulation in this overlapping area, such federal regulation would supersede the state regulation. This follows from the supremacy clause.

A much more troublesome issue arises concerning whether the states should be allowed to regulate by the Constitution in the upper area which "demands uniformity," if Congress by legislation is willing specifically to consent to such state regulation. This issue was destined to plague constitutional law for another hundred years after the *Cooley* case.

In the *Cooley* case it was the Court's position that Congress could not give power to the states

[*188*]

to regulate in the upper area—the area of exclusive federal power. This was the area of the "implied constitutional prohibition" against the states regulating. If the Constitution itself forbids such regulation, Congress could not grant the power to regulate. In the words of Justice Curtis in the *Cooley* opinion:

> "If the States were divested of the power to legislate on this subject by the grant of the commercial power to Congress, it is plain this [congressional] act could not confer upon them power thus to legislate. If the Constitution excluded the States from making any law regulating commerce, certainly Congress cannot regrant, or in any manner reconvey to the States that power. * * *" 53 U.S. (12 How.) at 318.

There must be further evaluation of this conclusion in the *Cooley* case later. But for the moment, let us note only that the *Cooley* case established a significant and yet pragmatic analysis of the delegated commerce power by recognizing an area of exclusive federal power, an area of overlapping power and, of course, an area of exclusive state power where the federal power does not extend at all. We have already analyzed how large or how small this area of exclusive state power is.

The basic *Cooley* approach continues to be used today. The Supreme Court regularly strikes

[*189*]

down state legislation regulating in the commerce field on the ground that it falls in the area where uniformity is demanded. There is an implied prohibition against the states regulating in the field of national interstate commerce.

One fairly recent case is of particular interest. It is Bibb v. Navajo Freight Lines, Inc., 359 U.S. 520 (1959). This case held that an Illinois statute requiring a certain kind of rear fender mudguard on trucks was unconstitutional because the Illinois mudguards were atypical and resulted in requiring trucks from other states to change their mudguards as they entered Illinois.

The holding itself is not particularly noteworthy. Illinois obviously was placing a heavy burden upon interstate commercial travel by its regulation. What is noteworthy is the fact that Justices Black and Douglas had persisted in earlier cases in claiming there should be no implied prohibition against the states regulating in the commerce field. It was their position that the states, unless they set out to discriminate against interstate commerce, should be allowed to regulate in any way they wish until Congress passes a statute stopping them. In other words, on our diagram their analysis would extend the area of overlap virtually all the way to the top of the diagram. State regulations, unless intended to discriminate against interstate commerce, would be

[*190*]

unrestricted by the Constitution in the area that the *Cooley* case had termed "national" interstate commerce.

But in the *Navajo Freight Lines* case, Justices Black and Douglas had to back away from their view. Indeed, Justice Douglas wrote the opinion for the Court, and Justice Black went along with it. Justice Douglas' concession was narrow, but nevertheless it was clearly there:

> "This is one of those cases—few in number —where local safety measures that are non-discriminatory place an unconstitutional burden on interstate commerce.   *   *   *"
> (359 U.S. at 529.)

The most recent cases still use the distinction between national and local interstate commerce and find that the Constitution bars state control in the field of national interstate commerce. Pike v. Bruce Church, Inc., 397 U.S. 137 (1970), held that Arizona cannot require that Arizona-grown fruit must be packed in Arizona before being shipped out of the state. In 1974, in Allenberg Cotton Co. v. Pittman, 419 U.S. 20, the Court found an unconstitutional burden on commerce in a Mississippi statute which prohibited a Tennessee buyer of cotton from using the courts in Mississippi to enforce cotton purchase contracts which he had made with Mississippi cotton growers.

[*191*]

Great Atlantic & Pac. Tea Co. v. Cottrell, 424 U.S. 366 (1976), is of particular importance. It held unconstitutional a Mississippi milk regulation which prohibited the importation into Mississippi of milk from other states unless the other states had agreed to accept Mississippi milk on a reciprocal basis. The Court was unanimous in holding that the free trade requirements of the United States Constitution, Article I, Section 10, Clause 2, forbid the state of Mississippi from barring milk that meets proper sanitary standards from coming into the state of Mississippi. If there were any problem of discrimination by other states against Mississippi milk, this problem should be corrected by a lawsuit brought against the other states. But Mississippi could not set itself up as having the power to regulate interstate commerce in milk on the ground that it wanted to insure a fair market for its milk.

The *Cottrell* case follows two significant earlier Supreme Court cases. Baldwin v. Seelig, Inc., 294 U.S. 511 (1935), held that New York State could not stop interstate importation of milk which had been purchased at a price lower than the price fixed by New York. In the reverse situation, H. P. Hood & Sons v. Du Mond, 336 U.S. 525 (1949), the Court held that New York State could not prohibit the exportation of milk produced in the state to other states on the ground

[*192*]

that the milk was needed in the New York state markets to avoid shortages. Both cases strongly stressed that the United States is a free trade area as compelled by the commerce clause and that no state is entitled to place itself in a "position of economic isolation." Even when a state wishes to preserve its natural resources for its own use first, the Court has held it may not do so. Pennsylvania's attempt to satisfy its domestic needs for natural gas before any was shipped out of the state was held unconstitutional in Pennsylvania v. West Virginia, 262 U.S. 553 (1923).

2. Congressional Consent to State Exercise of Power

In 1890 the Supreme Court began a modification of the Cooley v. Board of Wardens principle that if the regulation fell in the area of national interstate commerce, demanding uniformity, Congress could not consent to such regulation. In that year, the Court held in Leisy v. Hardin, 135 U.S. 100, that a state could not forbid the importation of intoxicating liquor into the state. This holding was good law and was consistent with the Cooley v. Board of Wardens case, and indeed is consistent with the Great A & P v. Cottrell case of 1976. The statute forbidding importation was state interference with national interstate commerce because it erected a trade barrier at the state line. But, in its opinion, the Court did a peculiar thing. Every time it said that the Constitution forbids the states from stopping the importation of whiskey, it added the words "unless Congress consents." This was a new idea, an idea contrary to the analysis of the Court in the *Cooley* case.

But Congress took the hint and in the same year passed the Wilson Act providing that once the liquor arrived and came to rest in a state it became subject to state law even though it still maintained its character as an import by being in "the original package" or otherwise. The Court sustained this consenting statute of Congress the next year in the case of In re Rahrer, 140 U.S. 545 (1891). The Court's opinion was quite narrow and still urged that Congress could not delegate its own powers nor enlarge those of the states. But the Court simply said that Congress had made its own law which was a uniform rule that the interstate character of the shipment ended as soon as it crossed the state line.

Logic is difficult to distill from this opinion; practicality reigns. In terms of our diagram, and despite what Chief Justice Fuller said in his opinion, the effect of the case was to enlarge the scope of state power by creating at least some area in which the states could act with congressional consent where they could not formerly act. In terms of our diagram this means the jagged line representing state power has been shifted upward to encompass more of the area of admitted federal power:

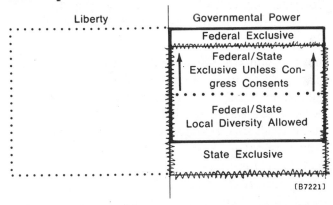

[B7221]

Twenty-two years after the *Rahrer* case, Congress passed the Webb-Kenyon Act prohibiting the introduction into any state of intoxicating liquor where the state by law prohibited such importation. This statute had the effect of authorizing a state to stop liquor at the state line. The Supreme Court could no longer call this simply a narrow modification of the constitutional rights established by the commerce clause. To allow a state totally to embargo a lawful commodity was obviously a sweeping authorization for a state to intrude in the regulation of national interstate commerce.

President Wilson had vetoed the Webb-Kenyon Act because his Attorney General said that it was unconstitutional, but Congress passed it over his veto. The Court upheld the act through the peculiar bookstrap device of not discussing the fundamental issue but simply saying it had already authorized a similar statute in the earlier case (In re Rahrer), even though that case was much narrower in its application! Even the Supreme Court "lifts itself by its own bootstraps" when necessary in the development of the law.

This same two-step process was then repeated with respect to the importation into the states of convict-made goods. Here there was no moral issue involved. The concern of the states was simply a matter of economics. The holdings of the cases involving convict-made goods amounted to a recognition that with congressional consent the states could set up economic barriers and embargos at the state line. Obviously, this was virtually total capitulation to allowing Congress by its consent to alter the constitutional distribution of the power to regulate commerce. The result is good. This flexibility in the distribution of powers between state and federal governments is important to the effective functioning of the federal system.

3. State Discriminatory Legislation and Congressional Consent

After these decisions, we were left with the recognition that, at least under the commerce power, the states' power to regulate in the field of interstate commerce was almost complete as long as Congress consented. One small area remained. The Court had always been adamant that when the states undertook to discriminate against interstate commerce then there was no doubt the implied prohibition of the Constitution was unalterable. An example of such a discrimination would be a case in which the state simply forbids the importation of milk produced in another state but, of course, allows the sale of locally produced milk within the state. We would have had such a discrimination in the instance of liquor if the states had been forbidding the importation into the state of liquor from other states, but had not been stringently regulating the sale of liquor produced locally. Of course, the situation in the cases discussed above was different from this hypothetical because those regulations were part of the then-spreading national interest in the prohibition of the use of intoxicating liquor, and the instances involved were instances of the states prohibiting the shipment into the state of liquor when they themselves were "dry." When we speak of discrimination we refer to a state favoring its local products and businesses by prohibiting competitive goods and services from coming in from other states.

Reserving for the federal government exclusively only the small area of discriminatory state regulation directed against interstate commerce, our diagram after the liquor and convict-made goods cases looks like this:

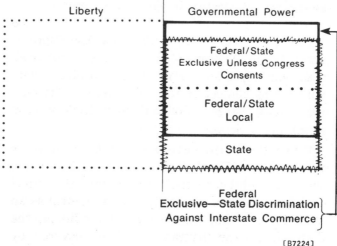

[B7224]

Even this small area of exclusive federal power where the states undertake to discriminate against interstate commerce was destined not to last. After the great decisions beginning with the *Jones and Laughlin Steel* case in 1937 which broadened the scope of the federal power over

[*198*]

commerce, we were left with a peculiar result concerning interstate businesses. All businesses which "affected commerce generally" (the test of the *Jones and Laughlin Steel* case) were subject to federal regulatory power under the commerce clause except for the insurance business. The reason for the exception was that an early case had held that the insurance business was not subject to regulation by Congress under the commerce clause because it was not interstate commerce. (Paul v. Virginia, 75 U.S. (8 Wall.) 168 (1868).) It was not until 1944 that the Supreme Court finally recognized that the insurance business, like other businesses which do affect commerce, was subject to federal control. The case was United States v. South-Eastern Underwriters Ass'n, 322 U.S. 533.

Given the broad decisions of the seven years preceding the *South-Eastern Underwriters* case, the Court obviously had to hold that the insurance business was subject to federal control as an industry affecting commerce. Accordingly, the Court found the insurance business covered by the Sherman Antitrust Act. But this holding created a host of other problems. Because the insurance business was one that had always been subjected to heavy governmental regulation and because it had been assumed from the 1868 *Paul* case that the insurance business was not subject to federal regulation, the extensive regulation of the insurance business had been carried out by state law.

So, at this point Congress was faced with two alternatives. Either it quickly had to enact a detailed code for the regulation of the insurance business throughout the United States, or it had to consent to the states engaging in regulation so that the state laws could continue to apply. The Congress chose the latter as the pragmatic alternative.

There was one serious constitutional issue built into the alternative Congress chose. Because the insurance business was highly regulated and was also continually subject to the states' serious scrutiny, many of the state laws regulating insurance discriminated against insurance companies from other states. There was no doubt that the states were engaging in highly discriminatory regulations against interstate commerce. But the Court had always said that Congress could not enable the states to discriminate against interstate commerce.

This very issue came to the Court two years later. In Prudential Insurance Co. v. Benjamin, 328 U.S. 408 (1946), the Supreme Court upheld state regulations in the insurance business which discriminated against interstate commerce but to which there was congressional consent. The constitutional development was then complete. The states have some power to engage in any kind of regulation in the commerce field. Yet, there remains the large area covering "national" interstate commerce which "demands uniformity of regulation." State regulation in this area will be struck down as unconstitutional—unless Congress has consented.

At the conclusion of this development, our diagram representing the power to regulate interstate commerce looks like this:

```
        Liberty              Governmental Power

                        Federal/State
                   Exclusively Federal as "Na-
                   tional" or Discriminatory,
                   Unless Congress Consents

                        Federal/State
                   State Can Control as
                   "Local" Until Congress
                        Stops It


                          State


                                              [B7225]
```

4. Constitutional Foundation for the Consent of Congress

How can this legerdemain be accomplished? The *Cooley* case said that if the Constitution forbids the states to have this power, Congress cannot alter constitutional power by mere consenting statutes. If the Constitution itself through an implied prohibition bars the states from regulating interstate commerce in certain ways, particularly discriminatorily, how can Congress by a mere statute change the Constitution? The Constitution can only be changed by amendment.

But this logical difficulty has not stopped the Court. Nor should it have done so. Careful reading of the Constitution shows that congressional consent to otherwise unconstitutional state regulation is not as startling an idea in constitutional theory as it first appears to be. There are several explicit prohibitions in the Constitution in which the words of the constitutional provision itself give Congress the power to consent to what otherwise is prohibited. The second clause of Section 10 of Article I of the Constitution prohibits a state laying export and import taxes "without the Consent of Congress." Note particularly that this provision is very close in its nature to state instrusions upon commerce. The third clause of the same article and section contains a whole list of prohibitions against the states, including the very important one concerning interstate compacts, and yet the states are prohibited from engaging in any of those activities only "without the Consent of Congress." In Article I, Section 9, there is a prohibition against any public official of the United States accepting any present from any foreign nation "without the Consent of Congress."

The lesson of these provisions is that congressional consent can be and is written into the Constitution as a means of altering the impact of the Constitution itself in certain particular instances. This similar kind of power has simply been recognized under the commerce clause. There is an implied prohibition against the states regulating national interstate commerce or regulating interstate commerce in an unduly burdensome or discriminatory way. If we make explicit this implied prohibition as it has developed and as it now exists, it would read:

> "The states are prohibited from regulating commerce in ways which are unduly burdensome or where national uniformity is required or where the effect is discriminatory, unless Congress consents."

This hypothetical provision simply takes the "implied prohibition" and makes it explicit in the words which could have appeared in the Constitution if it had been actually written. And these words are not shocking since we see elsewhere in the Constitution that Congress has been given a constitutional role to play by authorization through consent to exercises of power otherwise forbidden.

[*203*]

5. State Taxes on Interstate and Foreign Commerce

The Court has gone through a similar analytical development in evaluating the state power to tax in the field of interstate commerce. State attempts to discriminate have played a major role in this area. The temptations are seductive on a state to try to shift the tax burden to taxpayers outside its borders, since persons not in the state do not vote for the local legislators. The Court has regularly struck down these attempts as discriminatory. This shifting of the tax burden is "taxation without representation."

The problem is broader than this, however. Most of the readers of this book have run into its broader aspects at one time or another in connection with the sales tax. If you have moved an automobile from one state in which you paid a sales tax to another shortly after the car's purchase, you are well aware of this broader problem. So also are you aware of it if you have placed a mail order across state lines from a big store such as Sears, Roebuck, Montgomery Ward, and others.

The Court has simply had to make some "rules" as to which jurisdiction may tax interstate transactions. If it allowed both the sending and the receiving state to tax, the result would be what the Court calls "multiple taxation." While each state itself is not intending to discriminate under these circumstances, the overall effect of taxing the same transaction more than once discriminates against interstate commerce when compared with local transactions which are taxed only once. The general rule on the sales tax which has been developed is that the Court allows the receiving state to levy a use tax which is in the same amount and comparable to the sales tax collected in that state.

The rules unavoidably create problems in collecting such taxes. If you buy by direct mail order from an out-of-state mail order house that has no offices in your state, you do not pay a sales tax to the state of sale. While you may be liable for a use tax in your own state, it can be collected only if the goods are of a kind about which the state will learn, such as an automobile (because of the yearly license requirement).

The cases involving state taxation of interstate commerce are exceedingly complex. There is no intention here to analyze all of the nuances. But there should be brief mention of a few cases to show the complexity of the problems, and the general lines of their resolution by the Court.

How do you levy a property tax upon the rolling stock of a railroad or upon an interstate truck line? The Court says you are allowed to tax all the tangible property within the state plus the rolling stock which can be said to be located (have its home) within the state. Central R. R. Co. v. Pennsylvania, 370 U.S. 607 (1962). This principle worked fairly well with railroads and truck lines, although there was some double taxation. Then along came aircraft. The Court has come up with some exceedingly confusing formulations as to how aircraft is to be taxed and the best conclusion at the moment is that there remains a substantial potential for multiple taxation of aircraft because of the fact that airplanes are in or over so many states every day. Braniff Airways, Inc. v. Nebraska State Bd. of Equalization, 347 U.S. 590 (1954).

The problem of net income taxes derived from interstate commerce is also difficult. The courts have tended to approve formulas under which the state tax is based upon two or three factors which compare the local portion of the business to the entire nation-wide business enterprise. For example, the formula may include the gross dollar amount of business originating in the one state as compared to the entire enterprise, the number of employees in the one state compared to all the employees in the enterprise, and the amount of property of the corporation in the one state as compared to the amount of property throughout the entire enterprise. E. g., Butler Bros. v. McColgan, 315 U.S. 501 (1942). As long as these formulas are found to be reasonable by the Supreme Court, they will be upheld even though they could result in some slight measure of double taxation. They might also result in some slight measure of less than a full share of taxation for a business enterprise.

The issue in all these cases is burden upon interstate commerce. If the burden is substantial, the analogy is to "national" interstate commerce. If it is slight (and all taxation is some burden), then it is analogous to "local" interstate commerce.

Three recent Supreme Court cases show us the latest word in this complicated area of state sales, property, and income taxes. Standard Pressed Steel v. State of Washington Dep't of Revenue, 419 U.S. 560 (1975), a unanimous decision by the Supreme Court, upheld the Washington State business and occupation tax (comparable to a sales or use tax) on the gross receipts attributable to Washington from the business of a manufacturer located outside the state that supplied sophisticated fasteners (nuts and bolts) to Boeing aircraft. While the business had no office in Washington, it had skilled engineers who worked constantly with Boeing on its needs. In addition a team of engineers from the company came into the state and visited with Boeing for three days every six weeks. The orders themselves went directly out of the state, and the goods came directly by interstate shipment to the Boeing Company in Washington. The Court upheld the Washington gross receipts tax on the ground that there was no showing of a possibility of a multiple burden of this tax. Under the Court's previously existing rulings, the originating state would not be allowed to levy a gross receipts tax upon these goods moving out of the state, so the transaction would be carrying (in the words of another case) only "one tax worth" of burden.

Michelin Tire Corp. v. Wages, 423 U.S. 276 (1976), involved a property tax levied on Michelin tires stored in a warehouse after importation from outside the United States and awaiting shipment to wholesalers and retailers elsewhere. It was held that the state of Georgia could levy a property tax on the tires. This overruled the 1872 case of Low v. Austin, 80 U.S. (13 Wall.) 29, and the already substantially weakened "original package" doctrine. This doctrine had developed out of a misreading of Chief Justice Marshall's opinion in Brown v. Maryland, 25 U.S. (12 Wheat.) 419 (1827), in which Chief Justice Marshall had held for the Court that imports could not be subjected to local taxes until they were "commingled" with the mass of property of the state. He then simply gave as one illustration of goods before commingling—imported goods still in their "original package."

The *Michelin Tire* case which overruled the "original package" doctrine and allowed taxation of goods held in a warehouse awaiting sale does not fall under the commerce clause but falls under the clause prohibiting state taxation of imports from foreign countries. However, the development of the law with respect to the two clauses has been substantially the same, except perhaps somewhat more leeway has been allowed to the states to tax if the goods were imports from sister states rather than from foreign countries. The *Michelin* case is strong support for the Court's modern approach; the Court now makes interstate and foreign commerce "pay its own way" as long as it is not being burdened with multiple taxes.

The final case overrules an earlier doctrine which had been applied much more broadly than required by the discrimination situation out of which it arose. For many years, the Supreme Court had held that a tax "on the privilege" of doing an interstate business was unconstitutional. The earlier cases had solid foundation for such a holding; they involved taxes which were discriminatory, because similar local businesses were not equally taxed. Yet, the Court persisted in holding that a state tax on the "privilege" of engaging in interstate commerce was unconstitutional even when it was shown that a comparable tax was levied against intrastate businesses.

Finally, in 1977, the Court rejected its earlier practice of outlawing this form of tax. Instead, it began to look at the effect of the tax, just as it had been doing in other instances of state taxation of interstate commerce. The case is Complete Auto Transit v. Brady, 430 U.S. 274 (1977). It upheld the constitutionality of a Mississippi tax on the "privilege" of doing business in the state and levied on the gross receipts of the business. The company picked up General Motors cars from the railroad freight station at Jackson, Mississippi, and delivered them around the state. It was taxed for the privilege of doing business, although all of its business was interstate in the sense that it was completing the interstate journeys of the cars. The Court found the tax constitutional on the ground that it was not discriminatory. It saw that the only possible objection to the tax was that it was called a tax upon the "privilege" of engaging in interstate commerce. But, if the tax did not actually burden commerce, holding it invalid would be slavish to the mere form of the tax. The Court had been slavish to form in the prior case of Spector Motor Service, Inc. v. O'Connor, 340 U.S. 602 (1951), and that case was overruled.

Of course, any tax upon the privilege of engaging in an interstate business which has the effect of making the interstate business carry a heavier tax burden than competing intrastate businesses will still be struck down by the Court as discriminating against or unduly burdening interstate commerce. So also, any tax which by its nature can and will be levied in more than one state upon interstate transportation or upon an interstate transaction will be struck down as creating the possibility of a multiple tax burden on commerce.

Our conclusion is, therefore, that the analysis on state taxation follows the same diagram as does the analysis on state regulation in the commerce field at page 201. Undoubtedly, Congress can consent to burdensome and discriminatory taxes on interstate commerce. Its power to do so was upheld in the case mentioned earlier, Prudential Insurance Co. v. Benjamin. Yet absent congressional consent, in this broad area the states will not be allowed to levy taxes on interstate commerce, because the taxes are burdensome or because they discriminate. This is the "national" interstate area. Then there is the large area where the states may levy nondiscriminatory and nonburdensome taxes upon interstate commerce unless Congress stops them. This is the "local" interstate commerce area.

6. Congressional Consent to the Exercise of Other Federal Powers by the States

Finally brief mention is made of the issue as to whether Congress can consent to state control as to delegated powers other than the commerce power where congressional power is usually said to be "exclusive."

We know, for example, that the states can exercise war powers, otherwise deemed to be exclusively in the federal government, under the third clause of Section 10 of Article I of the Constitution, because this clause contains a specific provision concerning congressional consent. We also know that the power to coin money and to emit bills of credit or to enter into foreign agreements is absolute in the federal government, because there is a specific prohibition against these activities being undertaken by the states in the first clause of Section 10 of Article I of the Constitution. And in that clause there is no "consent of Congress" provision.

As to jurisdiction over admiralty and maritime matters, there have been decisions which hold that Congress cannot by consent broaden state power. That those earlier cases would still stand today if challenged is doubtful. There is no need for exclusivity with congressional consent. As to power over naturalization, Chief Justice Marshall himself referred to the naturalization of citizens as obviously an exclusive power of the federal government. It is also still generally assumed that the federal power over bankruptcies is exclusive.

Despite these presumably exclusive federal powers, the development of the law in the commerce field seems to indicate that at any time Congress has good reason to believe that there is a need to enable the exercise of power by the states in the area of one of its delegated powers, Congress would now be held to have the power to do so absent specific constitutional prohibition. The logical analysis of the earlier Cooley v. Board of Wardens case which held that Congress could not play a role in the reassignment of constitutional power has simply disappeared as a result of the development in the commerce field.

Under some of the federal powers, however, this consensual enlargement of the powers of the state would not happen casually; the Court would have to be convinced that this enabling legislation by Congress was strongly in the national interest. But if the national interest were to be shown, it is difficult now to see any further constitutional obstacle to Congress authorizing the states to exercise some of its otherwise exclusive powers. If this conclusion is correct, and we know that it is at least as far as the commerce power is concerned, our diagram will appear as it

[*213*]

did in its last version above. Let us look at it once again:

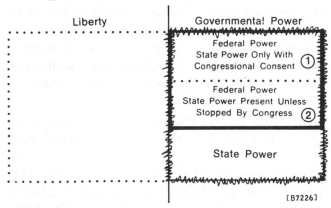

The upper area, numbered ①, shows the scope of the implied constitutional prohibition which bars state regulation or taxation where it is discriminatory or unduly burdensome or where there is a presumption that the exercise of power should be national and uniform. Here the Constitution by its own force prohibits the state exercise of power. Yet Congress can consent to the states exercising power which otherwise would be unconstitutional.

The middle area, numbered ②, is the area where state regulation or taxation is allowed by the Constitution, because the regulation does not discriminate or is not unduly burdensome or is presumed to be of a local nature not demanding national legislation or uniformity in legislation. But in this area, Congress has the power to block the exercise of state power to regulate or tax by legislating in conflict with the state regulation or taxation. Whenever there is a conflict between state and federal legislation, the supremacy clause, Article VII, Clause 2, prevails and the federal law is supreme.

There is an important admonition to be given at the conclusion of this analysis. While state power extends throughout the federal area of regulatory power under the commerce clause and under some other delegated powers also, it must be kept in mind that congressional consent is uncommon. Most of the cases involving state regulation and taxation in areas of federal delegated power involve instances where there is no congressional consent. Thus we have a steady stream of cases holding unconstitutional exercises of regulatory and taxing power by the states. These cases arise in the upper area, numbered ①, and there is no congressional consent. Usually, these exercises of state power fall as unconstitutional regulations or taxes by the states because of their interference with federal powers.

The practical impact of the Constitution on regulation and taxation by the states, therefore, is much more immediate and common than might be assumed from the ultimate breadth of state

power set out in the diagram. This fact bears repeating: Congress does not consent to these exercises of power by the states very often. The
states are on their own in most instances in
trying to avoid a holding of unconstitutonality on
the ground of a potential burden on a federal delegated power, or because the matter involved
should have been subject only to uniform national
legislation, or because the impact of the state
regulation or taxation is discriminatory.

The trend is not in the direction of federal consent to state regulation. The trend is toward the
Congress itself engaging in the regulation rather
than consenting to allow the states to regulate.
There has even been talk recently that Congress
should take over the regulation of the insurance
business. One clear and obvious example of the
Congress simply taking over virtually an entire
field of regulation is the regulation of labor-man-
agement relations under the National Labor Relations Act. Only very small businesses are exempted from the coverage of the federal statutes.
So the federal government, although sometimes
yielding to state regulation, more and more is undertaking regulation itself.

7. Conclusion

The overall theme of this chapter is that many
regulations and instances of taxation by the

states will be declared unconstitutional. We learned from the experience under the Articles of Confederation that a federal system will not work if the states can interfere with national policy decisions. So the Constitution upholds those national policy decisions by impliedly making unconstitutional state intrusions upon them. If a federal power can be substantially affected by a state, then the national government under the Constitution takes over the ultimate control of that particular area of state activity.

CHAPTER 7

THE VERBAL EXPRESSION OF CONSTITUTIONAL ANALYSIS

1. Summary of Verbal Analysis

Briefs and memoranda must be written and oral argument must be made on constitutional issues. It would be best not to initiate a brief or argument by saying: "Your Honor, now you see we start off with this great big box which contains all the governmental power there is. Then we saw off a large portion of that box, take those powers away from the government, and those are by definition constitutional liberties * * *" and so on! The purpose of the use of our box-diagram in this constitutional analysis has been to lead to understanding on the part of the reader. The concepts and analysis which have been pictured in the box-diagram must be conveyed verbally in legal writing and oral argument.

The aim of this chapter is to summarize our diagrammatic analysis by using words to convey the same meaning, and in the process of doing this to refer to four recent and noteworthy cases which lend themselves usefully to the analysis which has been presented in this book. But in this chapter the analysis will be done verbally, rather than in terms of the diagram.

First, let us lay the foundation of a verbal analysis. Liberty in the Constitution is defined as freedom from governmental restraint, not from intrusions upon freedom by other private individuals. There are three situations which are exceptions to this basic principle, situations in which a private citizen can invade the constitutional rights of another private citizen. The most prominent of these three situations is the "badge of slavery" analysis under the Thirteenth Amendment which has been extended to include substantial areas of racial discrimination by private citizens. The second is the important "right to travel" which is homeless in the Constitution but nevertheless clearly and firmly exists. The third is the federal election process. By implication, the holdings concerning this third situation indicate this would also mean other federal functions are subject to constitutional violation by private persons. For example, a private citizen's intrusion in the right of another private citizen to participate in a federal court or administrative hearing would be the same kind of constitutional interference with the right to participate in the federal government which has already been established in federal elections.

Under our constitutional system of judicial review, the courts define the scope of constitutional liberties and also have independent and inherent power to enforce the protection of those liberties. Congress has also played a substantial role, especially in recent years, in the protection of those liberties by creating criminal offenses and civil liability against those who interfere with constitutional rights. Under the basic definition of constitutional rights, this means that most instances of interference are caused by government officials taking action under their ostensible governmental authority.

There is one Supreme Court case which holds that Congress has the power to expand the definition of constitutional liberty in the Constitution. This case, however, is of doubtful validity since later cases involving the same kind of constitutional issue have refused to recognize a congressional power to alter the scope of constitutional liberties.

In the difficult and troublesome area of obscenity, the Court has recognized a power in the jury to define the scope of constitutional liberty, as free speech protections are opposed to governmental attempts to control obscenity. In other constitutional liberties, however, the Court has steadfastly refused to allow juries to define constitutional liberties. Thus, the issue of "clear and present danger" in cases involving alleged subversive speech is not submitted to the jury. Nor is the issue of whether a confession is coerced. Nor has there been any indication that the Court is willing to allow a jury to pass upon the validity of classifications under the currently most significant principle in constitutional liberty—equal protection of the laws.

We should be reminded, of course, that if the question is considered not to be justiciable, such as when the Court finds it to be "political," then the courts do not define the constitutional area of liberty. But this is a relatively minor aspect of the process of defining constitutional liberty. It is proper to conclude that in almost all instances the definition of the scope of constitutional liberty is a matter of interpretation and the application of the Constitution which, under our constitutional system, is accomplished by the courts under the principle of judicial review.

Once the liberty question is resolved in favor of the power of the government to regulate or tax, in our federal system we have the constitutional concept of distribution of powers between the federal and state governments. The federal government is a government of limited powers delegated to it by the Constitution. Except in foreign affairs, the federal government may not exercise any power without such a constitutional delegation of power to it. But in those areas where the federal government does have power, its power is supreme.

Relating federal power to state powers, where both governments have the power to control the same situations, has occasioned much complicated constitutional analysis in the past. The complications have been largely resolved into three relatively simple propositions:

1. There is an area of overlap between state and federal powers in most internal domestic matters, such as the commerce power and the power to tax. Where there is overlap, the states are allowed to regulate without congressional consent unless the state regulation is found to come in conflict with an existing federal law, or falls in an area where the federal government is found to have "occupied the field."

2. There is a further area where the Court will find state attempts to regulate and tax unconstitutional even though there is no showing that there is any conflict with federal policy or with a federal statute. These are the instances where state regulations are unduly burdensome upon matters which are subject to federal regulation. It could almost be said that

[*222*]

these are situations in which the lack of congressional activity indicates an affirmative congressional policy that there should be no regulation—state or federal.

3. In the area where the Court will find state regulation or taxation unconstitutional, even in the absence of any congressional action or establishment of policy, Congress may consent to state regulation or taxation, and under these circumstances the state legislative action will be upheld as constitutional.

The critical questions, then, which arise in the distribution of powers between the state and federal governments have to do with defining the scope of federal power, and then defining the circumstances in which states will be allowed to regulate and tax in the absence of congressional activity, as opposed to those areas in which the states will be held to be constitutionally forbidden to regulate and tax unless Congress affirmatively consents to such state governmental policy-making.

Finally, it deserves reemphasis that implicit in all cases involving distribution of powers between state and federal governments is a possible liberty issue. There no longer is any significant difference between the scope of constitutional liberties as they are protected against federal government intrusion and as they are protected against state government intrusion. Therefore, the first question in constitutional analysis is always whether the claim of unconstitutionality is resolved by a consideration of the liberty issue. If constitutional protection of liberty is found, then there is no remaining issue concerning distribution of powers between state and federal governments.

It is only in those cases where the constitutional issue concerning liberty has been resolved in favor of the power of government, state or federal, to engage in a particular kind of control that the issue of distribution of powers between state and federal governments arises. So even though problems of federal and state relationships are sometimes studied first as a matter of historical development, in every such case there is a lurking constitutional issue of liberty, which may or may not be a serious issue in that case.

2. The Verbal Analysis of Specific Constitutional Cases

In the remainder of this chapter, four cases are presented as a means of engaging in verbal case analysis of particularly noteworthy aspects of basic constitutional issues. In Cox v. State of Louisiana, 379 U.S. 536 (1965), a group of college students engaging in a civil rights demonstration

marched to the courthouse in Baton Rouge because some of their number were in jail at the
courthouse for participating in a prior demonstration. This demonstration was part of the
general sit-in demonstrations against restaurants
and other public facilities operated by private interests.

Cox participated in the demonstration and
spoke to the demonstrators at the end of the
march. He urged them to go from the courthouse to various restaurants and stores to engage
in sit-ins. Among other charges, Cox was convicted of breach of the peace. The facts which
the state urged justified the breach of the peace
conviction are set out in the quotation below
from the Court opinion.

The Court, in an opinion by Justice Goldberg,
made the following important and noteworthy
statement in commenting on the breach of the
peace conviction. As you read this statement,
consider its implications in the definition of and
explanation of constitutional liberty. At page
546 of the opinion the Court says:

> "The state argues * * * that while
> the demonstrators started out to be orderly,
> the loud cheering and clapping by the stu-
> dents in response to the singing from the jail
> converted the peaceful assembly into a riot-

ous one. The record, however, does not
support this assertion. It is true that the students, in response to the singing of their fel-
lows who were in custody, cheered and ap-
plauded. However, the meeting was an out-
door meeting and a key state witness testi-
fied that while the singing was loud, it was
not disorderly. There is, moreover, no indication that the mood of the students was
ever hostile, aggressive, or unfriendly. Our
conclusion that the entire meeting from the
beginning until its disbursal by tear gas was
orderly and not riotous is confirmed by a
film of the events taken by a television news
photographer, which was offered in evidence
as a state exhibit. We have viewed the film,
and it reveals that the students, though they
undoubtedly cheered and clapped, were well-
behaved throughout. *   *   *"

The Court then concluded that the First Amendment freedoms of speech and assembly as applied
to the states by the Fourteenth Amendment were
denied by convicting Cox for breach of the peace.
The conviction was reversed.

The above quotation is remarkable because it
demonstrates with complete clarity that in deciding a constitutional issue that turns upon the
facts of what happened, the Court feels not the
slightest necessity to accept conclusory fact-find-

ings of the lower courts. The constitutional dividing line between a state's power to punish breach of the peace and an individual's constitutional right of freedom of speech and assembly turns upon the facts of what happened. The Court itself, therefore, must draw the dividing line between constitutional liberty and governmental power. The Court itself must define the scope of the constitutional freedom of speech and assembly as against a claim that a breach of the peace occurred. So here we have a clear example of the Court substituting its own independent determination of what happened in a particular situation, totally refusing to take conclusory findings of fact made by the state court.

The basis of this holding may even be projected one step further. If the Court is convinced that facts were withheld or not fully developed in a record so that the Court cannot independently make its own determination as to what happened, it will reverse on a failure of procedures. The Court will not stand to have its independent power to determine constitutional issues as a question of law interfered with by findings of fact made by the judge or jury in the trial court.

Mathews v. Diaz, 426 U.S. 67 (1976), involved the issue of the constitutionality of a federal statute which limited participation by aliens in a federal medical insurance program only to those aliens who had had continuous residence in the United States for five years and had been admitted for permanent residence. The constitutionality of this statute was challenged on the ground that it discriminated against aliens.

The classification of alienage has been held a "suspect classification" which results in invidious discrimination which the state must justify to uphold. In this case, however, the Court held that the issue was discrimination among aliens because some aliens were entitled to claim these benefits and others were not. This is a facile approach, but it raises considerable doubt about the earlier Supreme Court holding that alienage was a suspect classification.

The noteworthy analysis in Justice Stevens' opinion for the Court, however, is contained in these words:

"For reasons long recognized as valid, the responsibility for regulating the relationship between the United States and our alien visitors has been committed to the political branches of the Federal Government. Since decisions in these matters may implicate our relations with foreign powers, and since a wide variety of classifications must be defined in the light of changing political and economic circumstances, such decisions are frequently of a character more appropriate to either the legislature or the executive than the judiciary. * * * Any rule of constitutional law that would inhibit the flexibility of the political branches of the government to respond to changing world conditions should be adopted only with the greatest caution. The reasons that preclude judicial review of political questions also dictate a narrow standard of review of decisions made by the Congress or the President in the area of immigration and naturalization. * * * In this case, since appellees have not identified a principled basis for prescribing a different standard than the one selected by Congress, they have, in effect, merely invited us to substitute our judgment for that of Congress in deciding which aliens shall be eligible to participate in the supplementary insurance program on the same conditions as citizens. We decline the invitation." At pp. 81, 84.

The analytical implication of this statement is found in the rather peculiar mixture of judicial abdication upon a liberty issue. When the Court does find a "political question," this means that the constitutional issue is being decided by another branch of the government. And that constitutional decision can have implications in the area of liberty. What the political question analysis means is that the scope of liberty as opposed to governmental power is being decided in that narrow classification of cases by the Congress or the President rather than by the courts.

But in this case the Court did not decide that this was a political question. This means that the Court knew and recognized that the ultimate constitutional issue concerning the individual liberties of these aliens who had not lived continuously in the United States for five years and had not been accepted as applicants for permanent residence were to be defined by the Court. Yet the Court found that this legislation lies in the area of governmental power in part, at least, by finding that it was not suitable for judicial decision.

The conclusion stated immediately above may be a slight overstatement. We could take these same words simply to mean that the Court has decided that there is no constitutional liberty here because this is so obviously a suitable area for legislative policy-making. The trouble with giving these words this rather mundane interpretation, however, is in recognizing that where individual liberties are concerned, policy questions are constitutional questions. So the Court must not lose sight of the fact that in reviewing policy determinations by the Congress, it must review them against a constitutional background and not just against a background of whether the congressional policy is good or bad.

The wording of the opinion is unusual, but is perhaps no more than an extreme statement of the common conclusion of the Court that once the constitutional issue is resolved in favor of governmental power, then the issue is one of policy where the Court will not intervene. In sum, the wording in this opinion does not sufficiently define the congressional policy issue as one which must be set against what is at least a fairly reasonable claim of constitutional liberty.

Raising questions concerning the analysis of the Court is not in any way to criticize the result in this case. The decision was a reasonable one and was unanimous.

California v. LaRue, 409 U.S. 109 (1972), contains a remarkable constitutional analysis in a narrow and restricted area. The case involved the constitutionality of state-wide rules adopted by the Department of Alcoholic Beverage Control in California which prohibited explicitly sexual live entertainment and films in all establishments licensed to dispense liquor by the drink. Reversing a lower federal court, the Supreme Court held the California regulations constitutional, even though the Court assumed that the rules prohibited some forms of presentation which would not be found constitutionally obscene and therefore would be protected as free speech.

Turn to and read the Twenty-First Amendment, which repealed nation-wide "Prohibition," the Eighteenth Amendment. The wording of that amendment seems quite clearly to be applicable only to the issue of the distribution of powers between the state and the federal governments. First it repeals the Eighteenth Amendment and at that point leaves the states in exactly the same position they were in before the Eighteenth Amendment was passed, as far as the Constitution is concerned. Then, in Section 2, it concerns itself solely with the federal power over commerce by authorizing an exception to the general rule that the states may not control "national" interstate commerce without congressional consent.

In other words, the Twenty-First Amendment was directed at the distribution of power between the state and federal governments. In terms it had nothing to do with individual liberties related to the use of intoxicating beverages since it returned the constitutional situation to that which existed before there was any attempt to control the sale of intoxicants in the Constitution.

Yet in the *LaRue* case, the Court relied heavily upon the proposition that "the broad sweep of the Twenty-First Amendment has been recognized as conferring something more than the normal state authority over public health, welfare, and morals." P. 114. It then goes on to discuss cases which do not establish this proposition but just properly recognize the importance of the Twenty-First Amendment to the distribution of powers between the state and federal governments.

The significant implication of these words is that the Twenty-First Amendment expanded the scope of state power as against the claim of freedom of speech, freedom of expression, and personal liberties. Would not those who adopted the amendment have been shocked to think that this was its implication? Further, it is obviously a dangerous implication, since the only way that state authority over public health, welfare, and morals can be expanded beyond its "normal state" is to intrude in the area of constitutional liberty. This means that insofar as the Court relied upon the Twenty-First Amendment, it was in terms expanding the scope of state power against the assertion of an important constitutional liberty.

This analysis was not necessary to the decision in the case. The Court later went on to point out that it might well be reasonable to conclude that the public sale of liquor and public sex shows do not mix very well in our society. This is a straightforward analysis which simply defines the scope of the constitutional liberty of free speech and expression in terms of a narrow restriction upon such expression in a certain situation where particular dangers to society are created. At an earlier time, you might very well have had a Court analysis finding a "clear and present danger" that this mixture would bring about public evils that the state had a right to prohibit.

But whether or not those words are appropriate in a nonsubversive case, the nature of the analysis does not change. It is a balancing of the limitations upon speech against the need for governmental control in particular areas. This is no more than the standard constitutional device of the Court defining the scope of constitutional liberty as against the assertions of the need for governmental power to control. Under this straightforward analysis, the decision is at least a reasonable one, even though there were three dissents. But it is troublesome constitutional analysis, indeed, to find that the Twenty-First Amendment has created an additional limitation upon free speech, even if only in a limited area.

Regents of the University of California v. Bakke, 98 S.Ct. 2733 (1978), came to the United States Supreme Court as a straightforward case involving constitutional liberty. Bakke, a member of the white race, claimed that the University of California Medical School engaged in reverse racial discrimination by favoring members of the black race in admission to the medical school. The case was of the greatest importance because it was the first case to give us a definitive holding on the critical issue of whether race can be taken into account in the nonremedial situation —in cases where there has been no prior constitutional violation by racial discrimination. It has been well-established, of course, that as a matter of remedying past racial discrimination, races can be counted and at least soft quotas can be set up. An earlier attempt to raise the reverse discrimination case in a nonremedy situation failed because the case had become moot. DeFunis v. Odegaard, 416 U.S. 312 (1974).

The particularly interesting aspect of the *Bakke* case for purposes of our constitutional analysis arose during oral argument. The argument was being pitched solely on the constitutional issue. But from the bench, the Court requested that the parties consider the statutory issue raised by the Civil Rights Act of 1964. Title VI, Section 601, of that act provides:

> "No person in the United States shall, on the ground of race, color, or national origin be excluded from participation in, be denied the benefits of, or be subjected to discrimination under any program or activity receiving federal financial assistance."

The California Medical Schools fall within this provision because they do receive federal financial assistance.

This request from the bench, with a later direction to the parties to file briefs on the statutory issue, immediately raised the possibility that the Court was thinking in terms of a discretionary policy issue. Stated in terms of constitutional liberty, this would mean that the Court would recognize the right to take race into account, at least in some nonremedy situations, but that also there could be a statutory policy specifically outlawing taking race into account at all in a nonremedy situation.

By making this alteration in the direction of the case, the Court opened the possibility of governmental policy control without running afoul of constitutional liberty, which would enable some favoritism on a racial basis or deny any favoritism on a racial basis in the straightforward nonremedy situation.

We have in this case two competing constitutional liberties. One is the constitutional liberty of blacks to be treated fairly in our society without discrimination, and this, they claim in the *Bakke* case, entails taking race into account to enable a more racially balanced admissions policy to the medical school. The competing constitutional right is the claim of Bakke that race cannot be used to deny him the important public opportunity to go to medical school by favoring a black applicant who is less qualified on whatever objective basis is used to admit to medical school, with the one exception that the applicant less qualified is black.

The case posed a difficult constitutional issue of balancing these two constitutional rights. But the Court in requesting argument on the impact of Title VI of the Civil Rights Act opened the possibility that these two competing constitutional rights are not directly opposed to each other but that there is an area where neither constitutional right comes into play as an area of governmental power where the government may create a policy which bars all consideration of race in certain situations but also can permit consideration of race in those same situations. This possibility comports with the analysis already set forth in such cases as *Moose Lodge*, at p. 108.

When the Supreme Court decided the case in June, 1978, Bakke's right to be admitted to the University of California Medical School was upheld by a 5-4 vote. Four of the five majority justices based their holding entirely upon the statutory provision mentioned above. They did not go into the issue of whether the statute could constitutionally have allowed race to be considered in the way that it had been considered in the *Bakke* facts. In other words, the conclusion of these four justices to ground the decision wholly on the statute avoided any consideration of the constitutional issue. While they, of necessity, recognized that the congressional statute is constitutional, they did not go into the question of whether a different congressional statute would be constitutional.

The fifth majority justice, Justice Powell, found a constitutional violation in the specific quota on a racial basis used by the California Medical School. But in so finding, he joined the dissenting justices in recognizing that the Constitution does leave room for the consideration of race as a factor in an admissions policy and does not outlaw affirmative action programs even in those cases where there has been no prior racial discrimination and the affirmative action program or the consideration of race is not for remedial purposes.

The four dissenting justices found neither a constitutional violation nor a violation of the congressional statute in the California program as it had been carried out.

So only one of the nine justices actually found a constitutional violation, a deprivation of constitutional liberty, to applicant Bakke. The other four justices upholding Bakke's claim found only that California had violated a valid congressional statute passed in the exercise of its power to control the expenditure of federal funds under the taxing and spending clause of Article I, Section 8, of the Constitution. Those four justices follow the analysis that results from the cases involving the outlawing of racial, religious, national origin, and sex discrimination in employment practices under the Civil Rights Act of 1964 and racial, religious, and national origin discrimination in choice of customers of various business enterprises found in the same statute. It is a statutory control of discrimination which is relied upon without regard to any possible constitutional liberty prohibiting such discrimination. Thus, the contrast between constitutional liberties involving race and governmental power to control racial relationships plays a highly significant role in the Supreme Court's decision in the *Bakke* case.

3. Conclusion

The use of our diagram has been for the purpose of making clearer the important distinctions which the Constitution draws between liberty issues and issues involving the distribution of power between the state and federal governments. These critical distinctions must be articulated in words for purposes of advocacy and the writing of decisions in constitutional cases. By its initial summary, and then by focusing upon four cases, the purpose of this chapter has been to change our analysis from a visual one to a verbal one, and we have done this to change the emphasis from understanding constitutional analysis to emphasis upon verbal explanation of constitutional analysis.

CHAPTER 8

THE "GOVERNMENT" AND THE CONSTITUTION

1. Intragovernmental and Intergovernmental Relationships

The core of the constitutional analysis through the first seven chapters of this book has been governmental relationships with citizens. We first considered those circumstances in which the government is barred from dealing with citizens in certain ways, and we call this "liberty." Then we considered the situations in which the government retains the power to regulate citizens' conduct, and we call this the area of "governmental power." We have completed the analysis of this basic constitutional structure.

The Constitution, however, serves another function. As a final inquiry we turn our attention to this other orientation. First, the Constitution had to set up a national government. It is elementary that ours is a government of "separation of powers." The relationships between and among the branches of the national government raise constitutional issues within the governmental structure itself. We shall take a brief look at those relationships at the end of this chapter.

Second, the establishment of a national government required setting up a federal system—"a rare and difficult scheme," as Chief Justice Marshall called it in the case of McCulloch v. Maryland, which will be discussed briefly. How do two different governments exist in the same geographical area? There are tensions and disputes as to the proper allocation of functions and powers between the two kinds of governments. These were considered in Chapters 5 and 6. But there also are tensions and disputes created by a government's direct impact upon the functioning of the other government. The constitutional protections which have been developed by the Supreme Court to lessen intergovernmental friction between the states and the national government will be considered as our first inquiry in this chapter.

Third, there is the matter of the interrelationship among the states themselves. There must be some dealings directly between and among states if our overall federal system is to work effectively. The Constitution speaks to this subject as well, and we shall consider it also.

We no longer use our diagram for analysis, although it will have some relevance at one point. The diagram is designed to set out the relationship between our governments and the citizens. This relationship inquires into what government can demand of its citizens by way of regulation and taxation and what the citizens can demand of government by way of the protection of constitutional liberties. In this final chapter, we are not concerned with the citizen-government relationship. We are concerned with government-government relationship. And this relationship does not fall within the scope of our diagrammatic analysis.

2.   Federal and State Governmental Relationships

Of the three subjects enumerated above, the one which has a long and substantial history of constitutional litigation is the second, the one involving the intergovernmental relationship question. This subject consists of the dealings between the federal government and the state governments as governmental entities. The second most important case in all American constitutional law (Marbury v. Madison being the first) is McCulloch v. Maryland, 17 U.S. (4 Wheat.) 316 (1819), which held unconstitutional a heavy and discriminatory Maryland state tax on the Baltimore branch of the Bank of the United States. The bank was owned and operated by the United States and carried out banking business in a retail sense, supplying banking services to individual customers. It disappeared from the national scene during the presidency of Andrew Jackson.

Chief Justice Marshall writing for the unanimous Supreme Court found that the Constitution impliedly prohibited a state levying a tax upon a federal governmental instrumentality. His reasoning was succinctly summarized in the words which Daniel Webster had used in argument (often misquoted by substituting "is" for "involves"): " * * * [T]he power to tax involves the power to destroy; * * *."

The Court opinion also discussed whether this was a reciprocal constitutional principle which would bar the federal government from levying taxes upon the states. Marshall refused to accept the reciprocal principle, because there is taxation without representation when the states tax the federal government since the federal government is not represented in the state legislatures. But when the federal government is taxing the states, there is representative taxation because the states are represented in the national Congress. Further, the Constitution requires that federal taxes be fairly apportioned so that no states can be singled out for disproportionate tax burden.

Over fifty years later, in Collector v. Day, 78 U.S. (11 Wall.) 113 (1871), the Court, nevertheless, made the tax immunity reciprocal. It held that there was also a prohibition upon the federal government levying taxes upon state owned and operated instrumentalities. We call this principle intergovernmental tax immunity.

For many years after the *Day* case, the Court viewed an income tax by one government upon a governmental employee of the other government as a tax on the government and forbidden by this doctrine of intergovernmental immunity. Indeed, Collector v. Day was such a case. Finally, however, in Graves v. New York ex rel. O'Keefe, 306 U.S. 466 (1939), the Court held that a tax on the income of a government employee was not to be considered a tax upon the source, the state instrumentality itself.

Many years ago the Court developed a distinction between the unique governmental functions of a state which may not be subjected to federal taxation and a general business or commercial enterprise engaged in by a state. In the latter instance, it was held that the state activity, being of a general business and commercial nature, is subject to the same kind of federal taxation to which it would be subject if it were not publicly owned. One of the leading cases on this principle is New York v. United States, 326 U.S. 572 (1946). In this case the Court held that a state-owned mineral water business could be taxed by the federal government. This distinction still persists.

With respect to the implied constitutional provision that prohibits the federal government from taxing state governmental entities and the state governments from taxing federal governmental entities, the Court never fell into the analysis which forbade the taxed government from consenting to the taxation, as the Court did in analyzing the implied prohibition of the commerce clause. Chief Justice Marshall recognized the right of the federal government to consent to state taxation in the first leading case, McCulloch v. Maryland. The federal government has from time to time consented to state taxation of federal governmental instrumentalities. While no state has ever been known to consent to federal taxation of a state instrumentality, there is no doubt that a state could consent.

Over the years the Supreme Court developed a different rule concerning the federal *regulation* (as opposed to taxation) of state governmental activity under one of the federal delegated powers, particularly the commerce clause. These cases held that the federal government was supreme in exercising the powers delegated specifically to it. The federal government was, therefore, held to have the power to regulate state governmental activities if these activities fell within the ambit of the federal regulatory power.

Sweeping generalizations of this doctrine were easy to fall into, and some recent cases tended to confirm them. As the Supreme Court has recently held, however, the doctrine was in part erroneous.

The earlier cases which held that Congress had plenary power under the commerce clause to regulate state instrumentalities were cases in which the federal regulation was being applied to state activities important to the state government but nevertheless comparable to business enterprises. A good example of such a case is California v. Taylor, 353 U.S. 553 (1957). The Court there decided that California, in owning and operating a railroad, had to comply with the Federal Safety Appliance Act in the couplings used on the cars.

Recent cases involving federal enforcement of civil rights against state governments were taken by some as strengthening the proposition that the federal government has plenary power to regulate state instrumentalities. South Carolina v. Katzenbach, 383 U.S. 301 (1966), upheld the constitutionality of provisions of the Voting Rights Act of 1965 which brought about federal intervention in the state administration of elections in cases where less than fifty percent of the eligible voters were registered in particular voting districts.

The purpose of the statute was to remedy disenfranchisement of minorities. Under these circumstances, the federal government took over the registration of voters in those districts and prohibited the states amending their election laws or redistricting without federal approval.

These provisions obviously constituted a major intrusion upon important governmental interests of the states. They were based, however, upon the constitutional prohibition against racial discrimination in elections. This is a prohibition which is a protection of liberty and not a matter of intergovernmental power between the state and federal governments. In the Voting Rights Act of 1965 the federal government was not regulating the states in an area where the states had governmental power. The states had no right to discriminate on a racial basis in their elections. The federal government was only providing certain enforcement for constitutional liberties. So this decision in no way supports the principle that the federal government may regulate state instrumentalities under its general power to regulate. Reference back to our diagram reveals this. This was a case involving the protection of liberty: it fell in the area of liberty on our diagram. But in this chapter, we are talking about cases which fall exclusively on the side of governmental power.

Similarly the provisions of the Civil Rights Act of 1964 which eliminated discrimination on the basis of race, color, religion, and national origin by governmental instrumentalities simply confirm the constitutional requirements that states may not discriminate on these grounds in their employment, educational, and regulatory activities.

One case, Maryland v. Wirtz, 392 U.S. 183 (1968), did come close to recognizing a federal right to interfere by regulation with state governmental (as opposed to commercial) activities by regulation where there were no liberty questions. This case upheld the application of the Fair Labor Standards Act, regulating minimum wages and maximum hours, to employees of state hospitals, schools, and other institutions. This application was an intrusion upon state governmental function only in these three named areas, but it obviously constituted an instance of Congress' directing the states to comply with the wage and hour provisions of the federal law in carrying out their own governmental functions.

In 1976, however, Maryland v. Wirtz was overruled by National League of Cities v. Usery, 426 U.S. 833. Congress in 1974 had broadened the Fair Labor Standards Act to cover all state employees. There was coverage even for fire protection and law enforcement personnel, but there were some partial exceptions for them. The Supreme Court declared this federal regulatory coverage of state employees unconstitutional in an opinion by Justice Rehnquist. Justices Brennan, White, and Marshall dissented.

Whether or not National League of Cities v. Usery is a correct or incorrect decision on its facts, and a good argument can be made for the proposition that there is no serious intrusion upon important government interests by the minimum requirements of the Fair Labor Standards Act, the principle is inescapably sound that there must be at some point an implied regulatory immunity of the states from federal regulation. If it is valid that the power to tax involves the power to destroy, it is even more valid that the power to regulate involves the power to destroy.

Assume, for example, that Congress decides· to extend the provisions of the National Labor Relations Act to state employees. This action would grant to the employees the right to organize into unions under federally supervised elections. It would require the state governments to bargain with the unions over wages and hours and working conditions, thereby usurping state legislative power with respect to these matters. This extension of federal law would legalize the right of public employees to strike, to picket, and to engage in other similar concerted activity. These rights would in turn mean that the employees would have the unrestricted right to engage in economic strikes of indefinite duration and that any attempt by the state to interfere with that right would be a violation of federal law. This kind of federal regulation must be viewed as impliedly prohibited by the Constitution when applied to state treatment of its own employees engaged in essential governmental functions.

Similar extreme examples could be multiplied. In one such example, the federal Congress could start telling states that they had to levy higher taxes and spend more money on highways, because their state highway policies burden interstate commerce. Since federal legislation under the supremacy clause overrules even a contrary state constitutional provision, the federal legislation would be supreme. Congress, therefore, cannot be viewed as having the power to legislate in ways which would interfere with the fundamental governmental activities of a state. The National League of Cities v. Usery case confirmed this inescapable principle.

So there is an intergovernmental tax immunity between the federal government and the states implied in the Constitution. Further, there is an intergovernmental regulatory immunity. It is implied insofar as the federal government undertakes to regulate the states, and it is explicit in the supremacy clause insofar as the states attempt to regulate the federal government.

3. The Relationships of the States With Each Other

Our third listed subject is the relationships of the states with each other. The constitutional reference for this subject is Article I, Section 10, providing "No state shall, without the Consent of Congress * * * enter into any Agreement or Compact with another state * * *." This constitutional provision is not followed literally. It was early recognized that states could make contracts with each other involving various issues but which did not need to be submitted to Congress. These may be simply agreements involving, for example, reciprocal recognition of professional qualifications for doctors and lawyers, the purchase and sale of property such as surplus buses, and other matters. In the case of Virginia v. Tennessee, 148 U.S. 503 (1893), the Court created the needed distinction by holding that the application of the compact clause is limited to agreements "directed to the formation of any combination tending to the increase of political power in the states, which may encroach upon or interfere with the just supremacy of the United States." 148 U.S. at 519.

A useful recent case involving the application of this principle is New Hampshire v. Maine, 426 U.S. 363 (1976). New Hampshire sued Maine as a matter of original jurisdiction in the Supreme Court seeking to resolve a minor boundary dispute. Before the trial of the case the states agreed upon a settlement and moved for a consent judgment. The Supreme Court held by a vote of 6-3 that the states could reach such an agreement without calling the congressional approval provisions of the compact clause into play. The Court saw no significant increase of political power in the states which might encroach upon or interfere with the supremacy of the United States.

The use of the compact power has been quite widespread, although it has not been made the subject of much publicity. The New York Port Authority is created under an interstate compact approved by Congress. Compacts have been used widely in the control of crime. Compacts are often used in establishing interstate rules concerning fishing and hunting. A little-known but important compact creates the Interstate Oil Com-

[*253*]

pact Commission which works on conservation and production quotas. There also have been compacts concerning flood control. The Colorado River Compact relates to the allocation of the river water.

The ultimate authority to interpret and apply interstate compacts has been held by the Supreme Court to be lodged in its own chambers. West Virginia v. Sims, 341 U.S. 22 (1951).

4. Relationships Among the Branches of the Federal Government

Our final subject, the first listed above, is the intragovernmental relationships among the branches of the federal government. Events involving these relationships have created current excitement in constitutional law. A decision of the Supreme Court brought down a President. United States v. Nixon, 418 U.S. 683 (1974), was decided on July 24, 1974. It concerned the issue of whether a grand jury investigating Watergate had the right to subpoena the tapes automatically recorded in President Nixon's office. The Court unanimously upheld the right of the grand jury to get the tapes. Within three weeks President Nixon resigned because the tapes showed he had been lying when he claimed lack of early knowledge of the story behind the Watergate burglary of the Democratic National Committee headquarters.

The case held that there was and is properly a claim of "privilege" on behalf of the President under our Constitution. The President does have an expectation of confidentiality with regard to his conversations and correspondence. Yet his discussions with his office staff, recorded automatically on tape in the Oval Office, were not protected by the privilege because the legitimate needs of the judicial process outweighed presidential privilege in this instance. Conceding that the confidentiality of the President's communications and activities must be given the greatest protection consistent with "the fair administration of justice," the Court said, nevertheless, the privilege cannot be absolute and unqualified. The subpoena for the tapes was issued in the enforcement of criminal statutes. The "generalized assertion of privilege must yield to the demonstrated, specific need for evidence in a pending criminal trial." 418 U.S. at 713.

Some have viewed this decision as inhibiting good government because it recognized the doctrine of presidential privilege for the first time. But the doctrine has had an ancient history in American constitutional law, and it would have been folly to have said that there was no privileged confidentiality in the Presidency. The critical point in the case was the refusal to allow President Nixon to hide behind a veil of confidentiality when criminal conduct in his office was being investigated. In so holding, the Court created a judicial domination over the most intimate and personal aspects of the Office of the Presidency.

Another recent decision gained prominence by establishing similar judicial domination over Congress. In the 1966 general election, Representative Adam Clayton Powell, Jr., of New York, was reelected to his seat in the House of Representatives. Pursuant to a resolution of the House, however, he was not permitted to take his seat. He and some residents in his district brought suit to force the House to accept him as the duly elected representative. The reason the House had refused to seat Representative Powell was because he had allegedly wrongfully diverted House funds for his personal use and had filed false reports on expenditures, both offenses having been committed at the preceding session of Congress.

The Supreme Court held in Powell v. McCormack, 395 U.S. 486 (1969), that the House of Representatives had no power to bar Representative Powell from taking his seat. The Court refused to accept the case as one involving a vote to expel, which is specifically provided for in the Constitution, even though the actual vote exceeded a two-thirds majority.

Until this case it had been generally assumed that matters involving the seating and expulsion of members of Congress were political questions in the hands of Congress itself and that the Court would not get involved. There had been some past instances in which the House of Representatives had refused to seat elected representatives, and no judicial challenge had been made.

These two cases, then, in stark and dramatic fashion, established the ultimate ascendency of the Supreme Court over the Executive and Legislative branches of the government.

One other recent case involving these difficult interrelationships is particularly significant. Buckley v. Valeo, 424 U.S. 1 (1976), challenged the constitutionality of various aspects of the comprehensive Federal Election Campaign Act of 1971 and 1974. One of the 1974 amendments created an eight-member Federal Election Commission, with primary responsibility for administering and enforcing the Election Act. The law provided that two members of the Commission were to be appointed by the President *Pro Tempore* of

the Senate and two more by the Speaker of the
House of Representatives. The remaining two
voting members were appointed by the President.
In addition, each of the six voting members had
to be confirmed by a majority of both Houses of
Congress. The other two members were *ex offi-
cio.*

The Supreme Court held these provisions of the
law unconstitutional on the ground that the Constitution unequivocally gives the power to appoint
federal officials to the President. The only congressional role in the appointment process is the
confirmation of higher appointments by the Senate. The Court found that the Congress could
not simply ignore and play fast and loose with
specific constitutional provisions setting out the
requirements for the appointment of federal officers.

5. Summary of Federal "Checks and Balances"

The separation of powers and the "checks and
balances" existing in our constitutional system
within the federal governmental structure are
known by all American citizens once they have
been exposed to civics lessons in public school.
But it is useful to recount them to remind ourselves that the Constitution by express provision

and by implication does define effectively the roles of the coordinate branches of the national government.

The following list is a generalization. No attempt is made to present in detail every intragovernmental power to check or control one branch by another. The main purpose of the list, besides serving as a reminder, is to emphasize the implied or unarticulated controls exercised by each branch of the government:

CONGRESS
Express Powers

1. Legislate. The power of Congress to legislate is sweeping. It should also be emphasized that this power to legislate includes budgetary control over both the Executive and the Courts and even includes substantial control authorized by the Constitution over the structure and jurisdiction of the federal judiciary.

2. Override presidential veto.

3. Impeach and remove from office the Executive and judicial officers.

4. Senatorial confirmation of high level executive and of judicial appointments.

Implied Powers

1. The Congress is the most intensely democratic branch of the government. Pragmatically it has extensive control over the activities of both the Executive and the Judiciary for this reason. The election returns are manifested in the makeup and also the activities of the Congress. Insofar as the Supreme Court "follows the election returns," and to some unmeasurable extent it does, Congress has this power of undefinable magnitude.

2. Investigate the carrying out of their responsibilities by the Executive and sometimes the Judiciary.

PRESIDENT

Express Powers

1. Veto.

2. Enforcement of the laws.

3. Appointment of executive and judicial officers.

4. The State of the Union Message and the recommendation of legislation to the Congress. The President has an ex-

plicit constitutional obligation to deliver a State of the Union Message and to recommend legislation. The recommendations of the President are obviously of extreme importance.

5.   Convene and adjourn Congress in certain circumstances.

Implied Powers

1.   Discretion in the enforcement of legislation. The President has broad discretion in deciding how hard he will push enforcement of some legislation and how weakly he will act in the enforcement of other legislation.

2.   Submit views on constitutional issues and on issues of statutory interpretation to the courts through the Department of Justice.

3.   Use the strength which flows from the prestige of the office. In the world as well as in the nation, the President is the leader. Not only does the "buck stop here," but the power of an effective President to influence the course of all national activity is without parallel and without measure.

COURTS

Express Powers

1. Interpret the laws of Congress to extract their meaning as applied to particular factual situations.

2. Settle controversies between private citizens and between citizens and their government.

Implied Powers

1. Interpret the Constitution and bind the Executive and Congressional branches of the government to the interpretation.

2. Judicial review of acts of the Executive, Legislative and Judicial branches to require compliance with the Constitution. This is the great power of constitutionalism, invented in the United States.

6. Conclusion

It is fitting that this book on the basic pattern of constitutional analysis end where it began with the statement of the power of judicial review in the federal courts. We now see how this principle actually gives the United States Supreme Court a certain preeminence over the other branches of government. Further, note that it is the Court itself which interprets this constitutional role for itself. Thus, the principle of judicial review is an anomaly; it consists of the Court's own leap into the role which the Constitution sets out for it, but which role is not fully contoured by the Constitution until the Court takes that leap.

The strength of this power of judicial review in the government structure and in all aspects of our nation's life is simply beyond full comprehension and full evaluation. The principle of judicial review is the very essence of constitutional law as we know it in this country because without it the courts would have no significant constitutional role at all. Not only does our Supreme Court have the power to allocate the distribution of governmental responsibilities among the various branches of the federal government and the power to define the scope of federal and state responsibilities, but the Court has that most critical power of all, the power to undergird and protect the great personal constitutional liberties. In a few words, this is what judicial review is all about.

*

APPENDIX A

LEADING CASE OUTLINE OF CONSTITUTIONAL LAW

I. THE PROCESS OF JUDICIAL REVIEW

1. Establishment of Judicial Review

The right of the United States Supreme Court to review legislative and executive acts of the federal government is found in Article III, Section 2, of the Constitution giving jurisdiction in the courts to "*all* cases" arising under the Constitution, and in the Supremacy Clause, Article VI, Clause 2. Marbury v. Madison, 5 U.S. (1 Cranch) 137 (1803).

The power of judicial review extends to the states, including the state courts. Martin v. Hunter's Lessee, 14 U.S. (1 Wheat.) 304 (1816).

2. Jurisdiction of the Supreme Court

Cases for review may reach the Supreme Court in three ways: (i) certification of a question from a lower federal court, (ii) appeal from state or federal court, (iii) the granting of a writ of certiorari to a state or federal court. Appeal is a matter of right and lies only in cases where (a) a state statute has been held invalid by a federal Court of Appeals, (b) where a state statute has been held constitutional as to the U. S. Constitution in a state court, (c) where a federal treaty or statute has been held unconstitutional in a state court, (d) in certain very limited situations where a three-judge federal court has heard the case in the first instance. Certiorari is discretionary and may be granted in any case involving the constitutionality of federal or state governmental action and the interpretation and application of federal law. 28 U.S.C.A. §§ 1253–1254, 1257.

3. The Case Requirement

A "case" requires that valuable legal rights asserted by the plaintiff are threatened by the defendant and will be determined by the decision. The question is one lending itself to judicial determination, and the relief sought is a definitive final adjudication of legal rights. Nashville, C. & St.L.Ry. v. Wallace, 288 U.S. 249 (1933).

Standing. In general, taxpayers do not have the right to raise issues involving federal spending because of the small and indefinite interest they have in the case. Frothingham v. Mellon, 262 U.S. 447 (1923). But taxpayers may raise issues concerning governmental spending in cases asserting violations of the "establishment clause" of the First Amendment (separation of church and state) because the claim here is that the spending exceeds specific constitutional limitations. Flast v. Cohen, 392 U.S. 83 (1968).

In general, plaintiffs cannot enforce the rights of others but must show their own valuable legal rights are threatened. Warth v. Seldin, 422 U.S. 490 (1975).

Exception is recognized when there is no way the person injured can raise the issue. Barrows v. Jackson, 346 U.S. 249 (1953).

Ripeness. Persons planning future political action cannot challenge the constitutionality of the Hatch Act prohibition on political action because the impact of the statute is still hypothetical. United Public Workers v. Mitchell, 330 U.S. 75 (1947).

A modern approach to standing, exemplified in a nonconstitutional case, holds that businesses threatened with competition under regulations broadening the power of banks to engage in auxiliary services can sue by showing "injury in fact, economic or otherwise," and showing they are "within the zone of interests" to be protected by the statute or the Constitution. Regulations authorizing banks to go into data processing in competition with data processing companies create standing for data processors to challenge the regulations. Ass'n of Data Processing Service Organizations v. Camp, 397 U.S. 150 (1970).

Mootness. In general, if the case is no longer threatening valuable rights, the Court will not hear it. A student challenging discriminatory admission policies in a law school had been admitted and was graduating at the time the case came for decision. The Court held the student could no longer raise the constitutional issue, lacking a class action suit on behalf of others, because of mootness. DeFunis v. Odegaard, 416 U.S. 312 (1974).

But when because of inexorable time factors, cases would always be moot, the Court will go ahead and decide the case, as in the decision holding pregnant women have a constitutional right to an abortion, with the cooperation of a physician, during the first trimester of pregnancy. Roe v. Wade, 410 U.S. 113 (1973).

4. Political Questions

A few categories of constitutional questions have been held to be nonjusticiable political questions. The Court explores the appropriateness of attributing finality to the action of the political departments and the lack of satisfactory criteria for judicial determination. The political questions are (i) foreign relations, (ii) dates of duration of hostilities, (iii) the constitutional amending power, (iv) the guaranty clause, guaranteeing a republican form of government. Baker v. Carr, 369 U.S. 186 (1962).

5. The Eleventh Amendment Limitation

The Eleventh Amendment does not forbid suits against public officials as suits against a state. This analysis is similar to the holdings that suits against public officials do not violate the concept of sovereign immunity (which prohibits suits against the government itself). Ex parte Young, 209 U.S. 123 (1908).

Congress has legislated to limit the exercise of the power to enjoin state officials in the Anti-Injunction Act, 28 U.S.C.A. § 2283.

6. Guides for Declining to Decide Constitutional Issues

Justice Brandeis in a concurring opinion listed a series of rules under which the Court would avoid passing upon constitutional questions even in cases "confessedly within its jurisdiction." The list is valuable but is defective because it mixes principles where the Court will hold it has no jurisdiction as well as those in which it will avoid passing on constitutional issues, even though it has jurisdiction. The list:

1. The Court will not pass upon the constitutionality of legislation in a friendly, nonadversary proceeding.

2. A question of constitutional law will not be anticipated in advance of the necessity of deciding it.

3. The Court will not formulate a rule of constitutional law broader than required by the precise facts.

4. The Court will not pass upon a constitutional question if there is an alternative ground for decision which will dispose of the case.

5. The Court will not pass upon the validity of a statute upon complaint of one who fails to show he or she is injured by its operation.

6. The Court will not pass upon the constitutionality of a statute at the instance of one who has availed himself or herself of its benefits.

7. The Court will not pass upon the constitutionality of a *federal* statute about which it has serious constitutional doubts if there is a fair construction of the statute which can avoid the constitutional issue. (As part of number 7, it is exceedingly important to recognize that the power to "interpret statutes to make them constitutional" in the United States Supreme Court is limited to federal statutes only. The state courts are the final authority on the interpretation of state statutes.)

These rules are from Justice Brandeis' concurring opinion in Ashwander v. TVA, 297 U.S. 288, 341 (1936).

II. CONSTITUTIONAL LIBERTY

1. The Nature of Liberty

"The very purpose of a Bill of Rights was to withdraw certain subjects from the vicissitudes of political controversy, to place them beyond the reach of majorities and officials and to establish them as legal principles to be applied by the courts. One's right to life, liberty, and property, to free speech, a free press, freedom of worship and assembly, and other fundamental rights may not be submitted to vote; they depend on the outcome of no elections." Justice Jackson for the Court in West Virginia State Board of Education v. Barnette, 319 U.S. 624 (1943).

2. Selective Incorporation of the Bill of Rights Into the Fourteenth Amendment

The Bill of Rights, as such, applies only to the federal government. Barron v. Mayor and City Council of Baltimore, 32 U.S. (7 Pet.) 243 (1833).

Incorporating various provisions of the Bill of Rights into the Fourteenth Amendment due process of law clause, making them applicable to the states, has been a gradual process carried out by judicial decision. The test to determine those provisions of the Bill of Rights to be incorporated is to incorporate those which are "implicit in a concept of ordered liberty." Palko v. Connecticut, 302 U.S. 319 (1937).

The first instance of "reading" a portion of the Bill of Rights into the Fourteenth Amendment, although technically avoiding the precise concept of incorporation, was that provision of the Fifth Amendment concerning the taking of private property for public use and requiring the payment of just compensation. Chicago B. & Q. R. R. v. Chicago, 166 U.S. 226 (1897).

The free speech provisions of the First Amendment were first recognized as being protected by the Fourteenth Amendment due process of law clause in Gitlow v. New York, 268 U.S. 652 (1925).

The freedom of religion embodied in the First Amendment was first held to be protected by the Fourteenth Amendment in Cantwell v. Connecticut, 310 U.S. 296 (1940).

The procedural protections contained in the Fourth, Fifth, Sixth, Seventh, and Eighth Amendments have gradually been held to be incorporated in the Fourteenth Amendment due process of law clause with two exceptions: the right to indictment by grand jury in the Fifth Amendment, and the right to jury trial in civil cases—the Seventh Amendment. The incorporation of these procedural requirements is summarized in Duncan v. Louisiana, 391 U.S. 145 (1968).

The only other remaining provisions of the Bill of Rights are the Second and Third Amendments. There has been no substantial constitutional litigation with respect to these two amendments, but it is generally assumed that if the issue arose they would be treated as binding upon the states as being included in the Fourteenth Amendment due process of law clause.

Reverse incorporation—there also has been an important instance of reverse incorporation. The Bill of Rights does not contain an "equal protection of the laws" clause. This Fourteenth Amendment provision has been read into the due process of law clause of the Fifth Amendment to make it applicable to the federal government. The leading case involved the unconstitutionality of racially segregated schools in the District of Columbia. Bolling v. Sharpe, 347 U.S. 497 (1954).

3. The State Action Requirement

In general, constitutional liberty is defined as freedom from the power of government to control. A private citizen stealing money from another private citizen is taking property without due process of law but there is no constitutional violation because the government did not do the taking. This is simply a crime, prohibited by the criminal law. So, with the exception noted below, liberty under our Constitution is defined as freedom from encroachments of governmental power. This principle was first stated in a case finding no constitutional violation in racial discrimination by hotels, public conveyances, and theaters, all privately owned. Because of the franchised monopolistic nature of public conveyances, the case is no longer good law with respect to them, but is still good law with respect to racial discrimination by privately owned hotels and theaters. Civil Rights Cases, 109 U.S. 3 (1883).

The current prohibition against discrimination on a racial basis in theaters, hotels, restaurants, and retail stores is not a constitutional right but is based upon the 1964 federal Civil Rights Act passed under the power to regulate interstate commerce. Heart of Atlanta Motel v. United States, 379 U.S. 241 (1964).

The Court early created the concept of acting "under color of law" under which it could be held that a public official acting in an unconstitutional way nevertheless constituted governmental action if the official was acting within the ostensible scope of his authority. Ex parte Virginia, 100 U.S. 339 (1880). This concept has also had important ramifications under civil rights statutes requiring acting "under color of law." In a suit for damages against Chicago police officers who had engaged in an illegal search of plaintiff's home, it was held the police officers were acting "under color of law," although acting illegally. Monroe v. Pape, 365 U.S. 167 (1961).

The failure of the government to act constitutes governmental action. The perpetuation by a state of a serious malapportionment of the legislature denies equal protection of the laws, even though there is no showing of any improper or discriminatory motive on the part of the state, but the matter was simply a case of the state's failing to act to protect individual rights. Baker v. Carr, 369 U.S. 186 (1962).

Private groups or individuals may be so clothed with governmental power that their actions constitute governmental action. The Democratic Party primaries, operated by the Party, were nevertheless held to constitute governmental action. Smith v. Allwright, 321 U.S. 649 (1944); Terry v. Adams, 345 U.S. 461 (1953).

State action can be found in the enforcement of private agreements to discriminate against those who are bound by such agreements but do not want to obey them. Enforcement of racially restrictive covenants on the sale or occupancy of residential property is state action. Shelley v. Kraemer, 334 U.S. 1 (1948). The line of cases led by Shelley v. Kraemer, however, must not be pushed to the conclusion that any governmental action enforcing a private desire to discriminate constitutes state action within the meaning of the Constitution. Enabling individuals to discriminate by means of enforcing laws, such as the trespass laws which enable private discrimination, does not constitute governmental action. But the line of cases involving the enforcement of private agreements opened the necessity for the modern development of the application of the state action concept described in the next paragraph.

The modern leading case on governmental action involves a restaurant located in a publicly owned parking garage. The restaurant discriminated on a racial basis. The Court abandoned traditional governmental action analysis. Instead, it held that the inquiry should be the extent to which the government is *involved in the discrimination* as opposed to the mere recognition that the government is always engaged in protecting citizens who may or may not be engaged in private discrimination on their own. Burton v. Wilmington Parking Authority, 365 U.S. 715 (1961).

Government has many connections with private discriminations. It licenses businesses. It administers scholarship programs in universities which have all kinds of improper discriminations if the state is found to be involved in the discrimination. It provides for and enforces the devolution of property on discriminatory grounds. The important leading case to contrast with Burton v. Wilmington Parking Authority involves a private club which discriminated on a racial basis with respect to its guest policy. The reason the case was close and difficult was because the club had a liquor license obtained from the state. There would have been no real problem if liquor licenses were readily available to all applicants. However, there was a restrictive policy on the issuance of liquor licenses which meant that obtaining such a license was somewhat akin to an enfranchisement by the state. In a close decision, however, the majority of the Court found that the state was not sufficiently involved in the discrimination to find governmental action. Moose Lodge v. Irvis, 407 U.S. 163 (1972).

A projection of *Moose Lodge,* reinforcing the majority's decision in that case, involves the licensing of radio and television stations. Here there is by the nature of the communications medium a restriction on the number of licenses which can be granted. But the government is not sufficiently involved in the actions of the broadcasters to force them to be treated as public agencies for free speech purposes. In the particular case, the Court upheld the right of a broadcaster to refuse to sell time for political broadcasts. The refusal was nondiscriminatory; it applied to all political groups. Columbia Broadcasting System v. Democratic National Committee, 412 U.S. 94 (1973).

4. Procedural Due Process of Law

The essence of procedural due process is fair criminal procedures, particularly fair trial. Local community attitudes and publicity may be such that it is impossible to give a fair trial in a particular community because no juror could vote for acquittal and continue to live in the community. Moore v. Dempsey, 261 U.S. 86 (1923).

Failure of a presiding judge in a criminal case to control publicity involving publishing pictures of the jury, public broadcast debates on guilt or innocence, publicity concerning police statements outside the court during the trial, coupled with failure to sequester the jury, can lead to a trial so prejudicial that a conviction must be reversed. Sheppard v. Maxwell, 384 U.S. 333 (1966).

The right to a jury trial is essential in criminal cases. Duncan v. Louisiana, 391 U.S. 145 (1968). A jury may consist of six or more persons. Williams v. Florida, 399 U.S. 78 (1970). A unanimous vote is not required in state cases but possibly is still required in federal cases. Apodaca v. Oregon, 406 U.S. 404 (1972).

A person who is in custody and is to be subjected to interrogation must be warned:

1. He has a right to remain silent and that anything he says can be used against him in court.

2. He has a right to have counsel present at the interrogation.

3. If he cannot obtain the assistance of counsel, and wishes a lawyer, a lawyer will be appointed to represent him.

Further, the person being interrogated has the right to break off the interrogation at any time. Miranda v. Arizona, 384 U.S. 436 (1966).

Where a person cannot obtain counsel because of poverty or for some other reason and imprisonment may result, defense counsel must be supplied, unless there is a clear and intelligent waiver. Argersinger v. Hamlin, 407 U.S. 25 (1972).

The right to have counsel supplied includes the right to have counsel pursue an appeal from a conviction. Douglas v. California, 372 U.S. 353 (1963). A transcript to enable an appeal must also be furnished. Griffin v. Illinois, 351 U.S. 12 (1956).

APPENDIX A

Evidence obtained against an accused improperly without a warrant or beyond the scope of a warrant falls under the exclusionary rule and will not be permitted to be introduced at trial. Mapp v. Ohio, 367 U.S. 643 (1961).

Warrants are required to authorize nonemergency inspection of residential and general commerical dwellings by health, fire, Occupational Health and Safety, and other inspectors without the owner's consent. But the warrants in general health and fire inspections may be area warrants covering all residences or businesses in a particular area of a community. Camara v. Municipal Court, 387 U.S. 523 (1967), and See v. Seattle, 387 U.S. 541 (1967); Marshall v. Barlow's, Inc., 98 S.Ct. 1816 (1978).

Searches incidental to a lawful arrest are permitted only of the arrestee's person and areas within his immediate reach or control. Chimel v. California, 395 U.S. 752 (1969).

Reversing prior authority, a telephone tap to enable overhearing telephone conversations is a "search and seizure" and evidence obtained by such a device is subject to the exclusionary rule. But proper authorization by warrant can be obtained for wiretapping. Katz v. United States, 389 U.S. 347 (1967).

Capital punishment is constitutional as not being cruel and unusual punishment. Retribution and possibility of deterrence are permissible considerations of policy. Capital punishment is constitutional where precautions are taken to insure that factors of aggravation and mitigation are taken into account, with the assessment of capital punishment being consistent because of the circumstances of the cases and not depending upon improper factors such as race, wealth, sex, etc. Gregg v. Georgia, 428 U.S. 153 (1976).

Due process of law is a growing and changing concept just as it was in Great Britain in the common law. The Constitution did not "crystallize into changeless form the procedure of 1789, * * *." Nashville, C. & St. L. Ry. v. Wallace, 288 U.S. 249, 264 (1933).

The question whether a change in the content of due process of law by the Court should be applied retroactively is determined by the application of three criteria:

1. The purpose to be served by the new standards.

2. The extent of the reliance by law enforcement authorities on the old standards.

3. The effect on the administration of justice of a retroactive application of new standards.

Thus, the change in the rule of the *Katz* case, above, is prospective only. Desist v. United States, 394 U.S. 244 (1969). The rule of the *Mapp* case, above, was applied retroactively to those cases which were still pending at the time of the decision. Ker v. State of California, 374 U.S. 23 (1963). But the *Mapp* rule was not applied in a case which had already been completed at the time of the *Mapp* decision. Linkletter v. Walker, 381 U.S. 618 (1965).

5. The Taking of Property

Necessary changes in society can detract from property values without the government being required to compensate for property taken. But when the government takes "too much," compensation must be paid. While the question is one of degree, it is not simply a percentage question but a weighing of the various factors and interests. Pennsylvania cannot by legislation take away the separate property interest of the right of "surface support" owned by coal mining companies rather than surface owners without paying for this taking of a separate interest in land. Pennsylvania Coal Co. v. Mahon, 260 U.S. 393 (1922).

Although a particular use of property was located in a particular place first, the inevitable encroachments of the more common uses of property can justify the abatement of this first use if its nature approaches that of a common law nuisance. As the city of Los Angeles spread, a clay mine and kiln could be prohibited and shut down without the payment of compensation, even though the prohibition resulted in a reduction in value of the property from $800,000 to $60,000. Hadacheck v. Sebastian, 239 U.S. 394 (1915). The same principle of no compensation was applied when cedar rust disease required the destruction of cedar trees because of apple orchards being started up in the vicinity. Miller v. Schoene, 276 U.S. 272 (1928).

Where the action of the government constitutes a sufficient intrusion upon the use of private property, compensation must be paid even though title is not taken. Aircraft in the flight patterns of an airport may be flying so low over adjacent property that a taking of a part of the value of that property has occurred and compensation must be paid. United States v. Causby, 328 U.S. 256 (1946); Griggs v. Allegheny County, 369 U.S. 84 (1962).

The normal activities of zoning property to separate residential from business areas are permissible governmental regulation without constituting a taking of property even though values in the properties affected are lessened. Euclid v. Ambler Realty Co., 272 U.S. 365 (1926). Residential property may be zoned to exclude lodging houses, boarding houses, and multiple dwelling houses from areas of one-family dwellings. Village of Belle Terre v. Boraas, 416 U.S. 1 (1974).

Historical zoning of Grand Central Station in New York City is constitutional without compensation even though it constitutes a severe financial loss to the owner who planned to build a fifty-five story building over the station or on the site of the station. Penn. Central Transportation Co. v. City of New York, 98 S.Ct. 2646 (1978).

It is a proper "public use" for a city to condemn an area, paying compensation, and then permit the private redevelopment of that urban area. Berman v. Parker, 348 U.S. 26 (1954).

6. Substantive Due Process of Law

From about 1900 to 1935, the Supreme Court developed a concept of substantive due process of law in the economic area as a means of holding unconstitutional various kinds of economic and social regulations. The most common formulation of this concept was "freedom to contract." In 1905, for example, the Supreme Court held unconstitutional under the freedom of contract concept a New York law which limited the workday of bakery employees to ten hours and the workweek to sixty hours. Lochner v. New York, 198 U.S. 45 (1905).

The Court began to break down this concept by holding, in 1934, that the State of New York could regulate the price of milk although dairying was not a traditional "public utility." Nebbia v. New York, 291 U.S. 502 (1934).

General business regulation today is found to have no constitutional impediment under an economic due process of law analysis. A state may require that a pharmacy must be operated by a licensed pharmacist. North Dakota State Board of Pharmacy v. Snyder's Drug Stores, 414 U.S. 156 (1973). Federal legislation providing benefits to coal miners suffering from "black lung disease" can constitutionally impose on operators the obligation to pay benefits to former employees who terminated their work before the act was passed. Usery v. Turner Elkhorn Mining Co., 428 U.S. 1 (1976).

The modern development of substantive due process of law has been denominated by the Supreme Court a "right to privacy." This name is a misnomer. It would better be described as a right of personal autonomy. The Court first began to define the constitutional foundation for the right as being contained in the penumbras of the First, Third, Fourth, Fifth (privilege against self-incrimination), and Ninth Amendments. Under this analysis, the Court upheld the constitutional right to obtain information concerning contraceptive devices and techniques. Griswold v. Connecticut, 381 U.S. 479 (1965).

The Court has abandoned the penumbra theory and accepted the theory of substantive due process under the Due Process of Law clauses of the Fifth and Fourteenth Amendments. Thus, there is a constitutional right for a pregnant woman to obtain an abortion with the cooperation of a physician during the first trimester of pregnancy. Roe v. Wade, 410 U.S. 113 (1973).

This right of personal freedom does not constitute a broad constitutional prohibition against the government keeping useful records concerning citizens. A state may record in a centralized computer file the names and addresses of all persons who have obtained prescription drugs for which there is both a lawful and an unlawful market. Whalen v. Roe, 429 U.S. 589 (1977). The police may issue a flyer to merchants warning of "active shoplifters" which includes in its list a person who has been charged with but never convicted of shoplifting. Paul v. Davis, 424 U.S. 693 (1976).

The major protections of personal freedoms other than the specific freedoms of free speech and freedom of religion are more commonly protected under the concept of equal protection of the laws, as set out in the next section.

7. Equal Protection of the Laws

Equal protection of the laws is a matter of the constitutional prohibition of discrimination between and among persons or other legal entities. It assumes there is no substantive constitutional right to which those claiming equal protection are entitled. But if some persons are given a particular advantage or disadvantage by the government it is discriminatory not to treat others similarly situated in the same way. For example, there is no constitutional right to a free public education. But if a free public education is given to some persons, it must be given to other persons without unreasonable discriminations. The Court will not demand that the money spent per pupil on education in one school district must exactly equal that in another district, but there must be a small enough difference in expenditures between and among districts to justify a holding that the difference is reasonable. San Antonio Independent School District v. Rodriguez, 411 U.S. 1 (1973).

The classic example of discrimination in violation of the equal protection clause is classification of persons based upon race. Separate but equal public facilities do not meet the constitutional requirement. Separate public schools based upon racial classification are unconstitutional. Brown

v. Board of Education of Topeka, 347 U.S. 483 (1954), 349 U.S. 294 (1955).

As a remedy for prior unconstitutional segregation in the public schools, race may be taken into account, and racial balance achieved by drawing school district lines and by requiring the busing of school children among schools. Swann v. Charlotte-Mecklenburg Board of Education, 402 U.S. 1 (1971).

Unconstitutional school segregation can result from school board policy even though not compelled by statute. The remedies for such unconstitutional government action are the same as in the instances where segregation is compelled by law. Keyes v. School District No. 1, Denver, 413 U.S. 189 (1973).

In establishing racial discrimination, there must be a showing that the law claimed to be racially discriminatory must have a "racially discriminatory purpose." A qualification test given to police applicants which has the effect of disqualifying more blacks than whites but which does not have a racially discriminatory purpose is not unconstitutional. Washington v. Davis, 426 U.S. 229 (1976). In determining whether a public school system discriminates on a racial basis, there also must be a finding of an intent to discriminate. Austin Independent School District v. United States, 429 U.S. 990 (1976).

In creating a remedy for racial discrimination in public schools, school districts which have not been guilty of racial discrimination cannot be forced to participate in remedying the unconstitutional discrimination of other school districts. Milliken v. Bradley, 418 U.S. 717 (1974).

The Constitution does not forbid the consideration of race as a factor together with other relevant factors in admission to schools and as a qualification to participate in governmental activities and does not prohibit affirmative action programs to achieve a general racial balance, even in those instances where the consideration of race and the affirmative programs are not remedial but are simply determined to be socially desirable. But a rigid racial quota can be forbidden by Congress and may be unconstitutional. Regents of the University of California v. Bakke, 98 S.Ct. 2733 (1978).

As part of the constitutional prohibition against racial discrimination, it is unconstitutional to prohibit racial intermarriage, discriminate on the basis of race in the selection of juries and the assessment of punishment for criminal conduct, and in the use of all public facilities and those private facilities which are in the nature of fulfilling a quasi-monopolistic public function. Race is denominated by the Supreme Court a "suspect classification" which means that the

Court terms racial discriminations "invidious" and will allow them to be maintained only with the showing of a "compelling state interest." McLaughlin v. Florida, 379 U.S. 184 (1964).

Although there is rhetoric of suspect classification in many opinions involving classifications based upon sex and wealth, the only other classification which has been held to be invidious, standing alone, is classification based upon alienage. Graham v. Richardson, 403 U.S. 365 (1971).

Where a classification burdens "constitutionally protected interests" (substantive constitutional rights), the "suspect classification" analysis also is used. This analysis is manifested in the constitutional "right to travel" which the Court has never attributed to any particular provision or provisions of the Constitution but recognizes as a substantive constitutional right. Classifications which impinge upon this right by limiting migration from state to state are unconstitutional. Placing an unduly long residence qualification upon the right of a new migrant to a state to be placed on the welfare rolls creates an invidious classification. Shapiro v. Thompson, 394 U.S. 618 (1969). So also for a state to place an unduly lengthy limitation upon the right to vote by persons moving from other states is unconstitutional. Dunn v. Blumstein, 405 U.S. 330 (1972).

By a close margin, the Court has avoided finding discrimination based upon sex a suspect classification. A number of cases have held various aspects of social legislation unconstitutional such as widows' rights being treated differently from widowers' rights or women's rights to claim husbands as dependents being treated differently from men's rights to claim wives as their dependents, but these cases have found these discriminations "unreasonable" and have not used a "compelling state interest" test. Frontiero v. Richardson, 411 U.S. 677 (1973).

The Court has occasionally upheld advantages based upon sex, as in a case involving a property tax exemption for widows not available to widowers. Kahn v. Shevin, 416 U.S. 351 (1974).

A disability insurance scheme which excludes from its coverage the physical disability resulting from normal pregnancy is not unconstitutional, thus leaving coverage under such schemes to statutory policy rather than constitutional requirement. Geduldig v. Aiello, 417 U.S. 484 (1974).

The traditional constitutional approach in equal protection cases has been a "two-tiered" approach. If the classification is not "suspect," then the Court assumes the state classification is reasonable and the person attacking the classification must prove unreasonableness or irrationality. If the classification is suspect, then the state must justify by showing a "compelling state interest." Dissatisfaction with the two-tiered approach in cases involving sex discrimination has led to the creation of a third level approach between the two extremes where the Court holds it must find sex classifications "serve important governmental objectives and are substantially related to the achievement of those objectives." A state law prohibiting the sale of 3.2 percentage beer to males under the age of 21 but allowing it to females to the age of 18 was held unconstitutional under this approach. Craig v. Boren, 429 U.S. 190 (1976).

Classifications based upon illegitimacy are not suspect. Those provisions of the Social Security Act that condition the eligibility of illegitimate children for surviving child's insurance benefits upon an actual showing of dependency were held constitutional. Mathews v. Lucas, 427 U.S. 495 (1976).

A test of reasonableness is applied in determining whether classifications based upon wealth or poverty are justifiable. It is unconstitutional to require the payment of filing fees for divorce in cases where persons cannot afford it. Boddie v. Connecticut, 401 U.S. 371 (1971). But it is not unconstitutional to require a payment of approximately the same fee by persons seeking voluntary bankruptcy. United States v. Kras, 409 U.S. 434 (1973).

The Court sometimes uses the language of "invidious" discrimination in voting cases on the ground that there is a constitutional right to vote. Actually, there is no constitutional right to vote, and the states still have the right to establish age (under 18) and reasonable residential qualifications in voting. The cases involving a "right to vote," then, actually involve classifications which are found to be unacceptable. So, the poll tax is unconstitutional because it discriminates against poor people in the right to vote. Harper v. Virginia State Board of Elections, 383 U.S. 663 (1966).

The Constitution requires a principle of "one-person, one-vote," an equal protection of the laws issue. Election districts must be reasonably equal in population to avoid dilution of the strength of each individual vote, and each house of a state legislature must be apportioned according to population. Reynolds v. Sims, 377 U.S. 533 (1964).

The percentage of deviation from population equality of voting districts determines whether or not "a prima facie case of invidious discrimination" is made out. This approach is somewhat unusual because it makes the "suspect classification" analysis turn upon how distorted a classification is, a difference in degree rather than in kind. Gaffney v. Cummings, 412 U.S. 735 (1973).

The peculiar doctrine of "irrebuttable presumption" has been used in a few cases to avoid substantive due process or equal protection of the laws questions. Thus, a state statute requiring nonresidents enrolled in the state university to pay higher tuition with the additional requirement that a student entering the university as a nonresident cannot change to a resident status during attendance in the university was held to be unconstitutional as creating an "irrebuttable presumption" of nonresidence. Vlandis v. Kline, 412 U.S. 441 (1973). State laws requiring pregnant school teachers to withdraw from the classroom some months before the expected birth of the child and remain out of the classroom for a number of months after the birth of the child were held unconstitutional as creating an "irrebuttable presumption" of physical disability. Cleveland Board of Education v. LaFleur, 414 U.S. 632 (1974). A much more cogent analysis would be simply to evaluate the constitutionality of the statute as a substantive regulation under a due process of law or equal protection of the laws inquiry.

8. Statutory Enforcement of Constitutional Rights

42 U.S.C.A. § 1983 has become a major source of statutory authorization for civil rights actions brought by individuals to enforce those constitutional rights which involve governmental action. A suit against police for illegally entering a home and searching it states a cause of action under § 1983. Monroe v. Pape, 365 U.S. 167 (1961).

42 U.S.C.A. § 1982 creates a civil action against constitutionally prohibited racial discrimination whether or not state action is involved. The "badge of slavery" analysis of the Thirteenth Amendment, which does not require state action, authorizes a civil rights suit under § 1982 against those who discriminate on a racial basis in the sale and purchase of property. Jones v. Alfred H. Mayer Co., 392 U.S. 409 (1968).

Similarly, 42 U.S.C.A. § 1981 provides that with or without state action all persons shall have the same right to make or enforce contracts and have the full and equal benefit of all laws as against a claim of racial discrimination. A private school which holds itself out to the public generally and fulfills compulsory education requirements but discriminates on a racial basis is subject to a civil rights action for damages as interfering with the right to make and enforce contracts without discrimination. Runyon v. Mc-Crary, 427 U.S. 160 (1976).

One Supreme Court case holds that Congress may alter the scope of the Fourteenth Amendment by a statute passed under its enforcement power in § 5 of the amendment. The holding is that Congress may prohibit as unconstitutional literacy tests for voting even though the literacy tests which do not discriminate in violation of the Constitution are otherwise constitutionally valid. The stated basis for this holding was that Congress may alter the substantive content of the Fourteenth Amendment by statute. Katzenbach v. Morgan, 384 U.S. 641 (1966).

The case in the preceding paragraph is of doubtful validity although not specifically overruled. In a clear opportunity to recognize that by the Voting Rights Act Amendments of 1970 Congress had the constitutional power to require the age qualification for voting in state elections be set no higher than 18 years of age, the Court instead held that Congress did not have that power. Oregon v. Mitchell, 400 U.S. 112 (1970). The minimum voting age was reduced to 18 later by the adoption of the Twenty-Sixth Amendment.

9. Freedom of Speech and Press

The core issue in free speech is the extent to which a person will be allowed to criticize the government, even to the point of advocating its overthrow. The constitutional test for evaluating subversive advocacy is whether the words used are of such a nature as to create a "clear and present danger" that they will bring about the substantive evils that the government has a right to prevent. It is recognized the issue is one of proximity and degree. The case creating the test upheld the power of the government to punish a person for sending out circulars calculated to cause insubordination in the armed services and obstruction to the draft. Schenck v. United States, 249 U.S. 47 (1919).

The clear and present danger test was refined in the case involving the prosecution of the top members of the Communist Party under the Smith Act for teaching and acting toward overthrow of the government. The clear and present danger test is to be applied in each case by evaluating whether the gravity of the evil, discounted by its improbability, justifies the invasion of free speech as necessary to avoid the danger. Dennis v. United States, 341 U.S. 494 (1951).

Membership in an alleged subversive organization can be made an offense unprotected by free speech only if the individual is aware of the subversive goals of the group and is an active participant in attempting to achieve those goals. Scales v. United States, 367 U.S. 203 (1961).

The requirement that for a person to lose the protections of free speech he or she must be an active participant in the illegal goals has specific relevance to instances involving requirements that public officials or those wishing to obtain public benefits must take oaths or give information concerning membership in organizations. Such is the rule in required loyalty oaths of public employees, Elfbrandt v. Russell, 384 U.S. 11 (1966), in cases involving admission to the bar, Baird v. Arizona, 401 U.S. 1 (1971), and where an organization is seeking access to the ballot as against the claim that it is engaged in subversive advocacy, Communist Party of Indiana v. Whitcomb, 414 U.S. 441 (1974).

It has been urged by some that the Supreme Court weakened the clear and present danger test as applied to subversive advocacy in a case involving advocacy by members of the Ku Klux Klan of a march on Washington which also included vague threats of illegal activity. Such a conclusion is an overstatement of the importance of the case because the Court found specifically that neither the indictment nor the trial judge's instructions to the jury in any way made a distinction between mere advocacy as distinguished from "incitement to imminent lawless action." Brandenburg v. Ohio, 395 U.S. 444 (1969).

Outside the area of subversive advocacy, the Court frequently used to talk in terms of a clear and present danger test but has largely dropped use of these words. However, when the issue is specifically one of advocacy of unlawful conduct, even though the conduct is not related to possible subversion, the clear and present danger approach still exists. Thus, where a labor union is engaged in picketing and the purpose of the picketing is to get the employer to violate the antitrust laws, the Court found a clear and present danger which justified the abatement of the picketing. The Court assumed that picketing because of its effectiveness virtually automatically constitutes a clear danger that it would bring about the particular result sought. So the only issue is whether the result sought is serious enough to abate the demonstration. Giboney v. Empire Storage and Ice Co., 336 U.S. 490 (1949).

There is a constitutional right to remain anonymous in political advocacy when exposure of views discourages effective advocacy. A southern state cannot constitutionally require the publication of the state-wide membership list of the National Association for the Advancement of Colored People since it would bring social recriminations and pressures upon the members. NAACP v. Alabama, 357 U.S. 449 (1958).

In contrast, the Constitution does not forbid requiring persons making contributions to political campaigns of $10 or more being revealed by records showing their names and addresses. Justification for the requirement is the elimination of corruption and the appearance of corruption by influencing candidates through contributions. Buckley v. Valeo, 424 U.S. 1 (1976).

It is constitutional to place upper limits on the amount of contributions from a particular individual to a particular candidate in an election. But it is unconstitutional to place a limitation upon the total amount spent by a candidate in an election. Buckley v. Valeo, 424 U.S. 1 (1976).

The government may prohibit nonpartisan government workers from engaging in overt partisan political activity on behalf of particular candidates or particular political viewpoints. United Public Workers v. Mitchell, 330 U.S. 75 (1947).

The Constitution allows substantial range for legislative committees to question citizens about their political affiliations which may be of a subversive nature so long as the questioning is limited to the particular relationships of the citizen testifying before the congressional committee. Barenblatt v. United States, 360 U.S. 109 (1959).

Publications criticizing public officials, although false, are constitutionally privileged from a claim of libel unless published maliciously (knowing that they are false or published in reckless disregard for the truth). New York Times Co. v. Sullivan, 376 U.S. 254 (1964).

"False light" cases arise when a private citizen becomes the central focus of a news event. False reports bring into play the New York Times Co. v. Sullivan standard and untruthful reports cannot be made the basis of liability absent a showing of knowing or reckless falsity. Time, Inc. v. Hill, 385 U.S. 374 (1967).

Private citizens who are in the public eye because of wealth or family connections may sue for libel for false news reports, when the news is not a major event, even though not malicious, but the constitution limits recovery to actual damages. A *Time* magazine story which falsely reported the grounds for a divorce in the wealthy industrial Firestone family gave rise to damages for libel without proof of intentional falsehood or reckless disregard for the truth. Time, Inc. v. Firestone, 424 U.S. 448 (1976). A lawyer who is involved in a widely publicized case does not thereby become a public official nor the central figure in a major news event and can recover for libel without a showing of malice in the false report. Gertz v. Robert Welch, Inc., 418 U.S. 323 (1974).

Of particular concern is "prior restraint" upon publication. Even though the publication of particular material may be unlawful, rarely will its publication be enjoined when it contains any element of free speech advocacy. The Constitution forbids an injunction against publication of the "Pentagon Papers" stolen from the files of the Department of Defense and given secretly to the *New York Times* and the *Washington Post* even though it was assumed that publication of the papers was illegal. A majority of the Court did not rule out the possibility of enjoining the publication of such papers with an adequate showing of sufficient danger to human life or to national security, but the Court was unwilling to find such a sufficient threat in the content of the Pentagon Papers. New York Times Co. v. United States, 403 U.S. 713 (1971).

The Court has always viewed with great concern as prior restraint any governmental attempt to require sidewalk pamphleteers or street corner speakers to obtain permits before they can engage in public activity. Lovell v. Griffin, 303 U. S. 444 (1938).

The Constitution does permit prior restraint upon the exhibition of motion pictures (censorship) with the additional requirements that: (1) the burden of proving the film is not protected free speech rests upon the government,

(2) there must be an expeditious review of the motion picture, and (3) the final determination to prohibit its exhibition must be judicial. Freedman v. Maryland, 380 U.S. 51 (1965). Although an unequivocal holding is lacking, it is almost certain that a similar censorship system for printed material would not be constitutional. Bantam Books, Inc. v. Sullivan, 372 U.S. 58 (1963).

While the press is the major purveyor of speech which is constitutionally protected, the business and commercial aspects of the press can be controlled by the government. A state may exact nondiscriminatory taxes from the press. Grosjean v. American Press Co., 297 U.S. 233 (1936). The press is also subject to labor laws. Associated Press v. NLRB, 301 U.S. 103 (1937).

Broadcasting facilities, because of the limited availability of wave lengths, are licensed by the federal government, and the federal government has a measure of control over broadcast content under a "public interest" standard. So it is constitutional to have a fairness doctrine which gives persons attacked the opportunity to respond, and also a general regulation of political editorializing. Red Lion Broadcasting Co. v. FCC, 395 U.S. 367 (1969). In contrast, the government cannot have an "equal space to reply" doctrine applicable to the press. Miami Herald Publishing Co. v. Tornillo, 418 U.S. 241 (1974).

Although broadcasting facilities are subject to governmental licensing with some restriction on content because of the lack of availability of facilities to all persons, the Court treats as protected free speech the general right of broadcasting facilities to engage in political advocacy or refrain from engaging in political advocacy. The refusal of the Columbia Broadcasting System to sell broadcast time to any political group or for any political cause is constitutional. Columbia Broadcasting System, Inc. v. Democratic National Committee, 412 U.S. 94 (1973).

Constitutionally valid restrictions on the press include requiring that published help wanted ads not carry a sex classification, Pittsburgh Press Co. v. Pittsburgh Commission on Human Relations, 413 U.S. 376 (1973); newspapers are not constitutionally protected from revealing the sources of news stories in situations where they are reporting criminal conduct, Branzburg v. Hayes, 408 U.S. 665 (1972); and courts can place reasonable limitations upon publicity surrounding trials to preserve a right to a fair trial, but a flat prohibition against reporting a confession by the accused where the confession was referred to in open court is not constitutional. Nebraska Press Ass'n v. Stuart, 427 U.S. 539 (1976).

Public advocacy by speeches and demonstrations on the public streets, while generally protected, can be so inciting to immediate violence that they can be prohibited. Feiner v. New York, 340 U.S. 315 (1951). This case is subject to substantial limitation, although not specifically overruled, where a peaceful demonstration inciting others to violence could not be abated on the general ground that the demonstrators had engaged in "disorderly conduct." Gregory v. City of Chicago, 394 U.S. 111 (1969).

Fighting words in face-to-face confrontation on the street may be constitutionally prohibited. Where a person called a policeman a "goddamned racketeer" and a "damned Fascist," the Court upheld the conviction on the ground these were fighting words. Chaplinsky v. New Hampshire, 315 U.S. 568 (1942).

The Court has gone to extremes to protect the right of individual citizens to display words or signs which are offensive to other people. A person wearing in the Los Angeles County Courthouse a T-shirt carrying the legend "Fuck the Draft" was held to be engaged in constitutionally privileged free speech. Cohen v. California, 403 U.S. 15 (1971).

An attempt to control nudity on the screen in drive-in motion picture theaters where the screens were visible from public streets outside the theaters was held to be unconstitutional on the ground that the statute was not sufficiently specific, although the opinion makes it very difficult to draft a statute which, short of actual obscenity, could be specific enough to prevent such an intrusive public exhibition. Erznoznik v. City of Jacksonville, 422 U.S. 205 (1975).

Wearing black armbands as a matter of specific political advocacy by students in a public high school was constitutionally privileged. Tinker v. Des Moines School District, 393 U.S. 503 (1969).

Displaying the American flag upside down from the window of an apartment on private property, with a peace symbol attached to the front and back of the flag, was held constitutionally privileged in Spence v. Washington, 418 U.S. 405 (1974).

The burning of a Selective Service registration certificate on the steps of a courthouse in the presence of a sizeable crowd was not constitutionally privileged. The government has the right to protect the integrity of Selective Service registration certificates and to require that registrants carry them at all times for the purpose of being able to act quickly in a military emergency. United States v. O'Brien, 391 U.S. 367 (1968).

Obscenity is not constitutionally protected free speech. The constitutional test of obscenity is: "(a) whether 'the average person applying contemporary community standards' would find that the work, taken as a whole, appeals to the prurient interest, * * * (b) whether the work depicts or describes, in a patently offensive way, sexual conduct specifically defined by the applicable state law; and (c) whether the work, taken as a whole, lacks serious literary, artistic, political, or scientific value." The issue is submitted to a jury under these standards. Miller v. California, 413 U.S. 15, 24 (1973).

If a jury makes too unreasonable a determination of obscenity, as a jury did in Georgia in finding the film "Carnal Knowledge" obscene, the courts will reverse the obscenity determination on the ground that the particular publication cannot be obscene under the *Miller* standards. Jenkins v. Georgia, 418 U.S. 153 (1974).

While the Court has several times said that obscene materials are not constitutionally protected free speech, the Court held otherwise in a case where an individual was prosecuted for having obscene materials in his home. It was held that under those circumstances the materials, although obscene, were constitutionally protected as free speech. Stanley v. Georgia, 394 U.S. 557 (1969). But the right to have obscene materials

in the home does not include the right to purchase them, transport them, or import them.
United States v. Twelve 200-Ft. Reels, 413 U.S.
123 (1973).

Important to an understanding of free speech
has been the common use of the concept of a statute being "void for vagueness" as a means of
avoiding a decision whether a particular attempt
to control free speech is unconstitutional. One of
many such examples involves the validity of an
ordinance which prohibits three or more persons
assembling on a sidewalk and "conducting themselves in a manner annoying to persons passing
by. * * *" This ordinance was held uncon-
stitutionally vague in Coates v. Cincinnati, 402
U.S. 611 (1971).

10. Freedom of Religion and Separation of Church and State

Freedom of religion is an essential aspect of
personal liberty, comparable to freedom of
speech. The concept of "establishment of religion," which is more popularly known as the
"separation of church and state," is a development of our own Constitution, and is not considered essential to personal liberty in most countries of the world. While recognizing the validity
of the "wall of separation" concept, the Court upheld the right to spend public money to supply

bus transportation to school children going to private religious schools as well as public schools. The finding was that the purpose of this expenditure was to protect the health and safety of the children, and was not to subsidize the schools. Everson v. Board of Education, 330 U.S. 1 (1947).

The furnishing of secular textbooks to private religious schools is constitutional. Board of Education v. Allen, 392 U.S. 236 (1968).

Supplementing teachers' salaries, even though only for teachers of secular subjects, is unconstitutional. In the case so holding, the Court created a threefold test which requires that the governmental expenditure (1) must have a secular legislative purpose, (2) its principal or primary effect must be one that neither advances nor inhibits religion, and (3) must not foster an excessive governmental entanglement with religion. Supplementing the salaries of school teachers violates the third principle by fostering entanglement because of the necessity of monitoring the teaching. Lemon v. Kurtzman, 403 U.S. 602 (1971).

Granting of government funds to religious schools for "auxiliary services," such as field trips, counselling, and testing violates separation of church and state. Meek v. Pittenger, 421 U.S. 349 (1975).

Tuition grants for children to attend private religious schools are unconstitutional. Committee for Public Education and Religious Liberty v. Nyquist, 413 U.S. 756 (1973).

A distinction between aid to primary and secondary religious schools and aid to religious colleges and universities is maintained. Government funds may be supplied to religious colleges to build buildings which will be used wholly for secular purposes, Tilton v. Richardson, 403 U.S. 672 (1971), and noncategorical grants of aid to private religious colleges may be made so long as the funds are not used for "sectarian purposes." Roemer v. Board of Public Works, 426 U.S. 736 (1976).

Churches and religious schools may constitutionally be granted tax exemption along with many other nonprofit organizations. Walz v. Tax Commission, 397 U.S. 664 (1970).

A school district may have a "released time" period during regular school hours when children are released from their school requirements to go elsewhere for the restricted purpose of attending religious classes while the other children remain in the public schools. Zorach v. Clauson, 343 U. S. 306 (1952). There would be considerable doubt about the current validity of this decision if it were not for the fact that it has now been followed for twenty-five years, seemingly with little expansion and controversy.

Prescribed religious services opening the daily activities in public schools are unconstitutional even though students are permitted to be excused from such services. Holding a service which contains a prayer written by the school officials is unconstitutional. Engle v. Vitale, 370 U.S. 421 (1962). So also is the reading of verses from the *Bible,* or the holy scriptures of other religions. Abington School District v. Schempp, 374 U.S. 203 (1963).

Freedom of religion includes the right of school children to refuse to salute the flag in violation of their religious beliefs. West Virginia State Board of Education v. Barnette, 319 U.S. 624 (1943). Religious belief can justify refusal to meet state compulsory education requirements, at least where the refusal is based upon the established beliefs of an organized religious group which has high standards of personal values (the Amish). Wisconsin v. Yoder, 406 U.S. 205 (1972).

The practice of extreme religious beliefs such as polygamy can be outlawed. Reynolds v. United States, 98 U.S. 145 (1879).

The free exercise of religious beliefs comes into serious conflict with the principle of separation of

church and state where general governmental
regulation may either interfere with freedom of
religion or constitute a governmental establishment of religion. Statutes requiring businesses
to be closed on Sundays as a day of rest were
held not to violate separation of church and state
because it was concluded that the earlier connota-
tion of Sundays being a religious holiday has now
disappeared. McGowan v. Maryland, 366 U.S.
420 (1961). But requiring Sunday closing put a
serious financial burden upon a merchant who
was an orthodox Jew and could not remain open
on Saturday because of personal religious beliefs
and then was forbidden to remain open on Sunday because of governmental control. The Court
held, nevertheless, that this serious financial loss
was not an interference with the freedom of religion protected by the First Amendment. Further, making an exception for religious reasons
raises problems concerning an establishment of
religion. Braunfeld v. Brown, 366 U.S. 599
(1961).

There are some constitutional protections of
the freedom of religion of Sabbatarians, however.
A Sabbatarian whose religious belief forbade Saturday work was held entitled to unemployment
compensation even though this gave an advantage to her and other Sabbatarians since other
persons were not allowed to refuse employment

on Saturdays. Some justices took the position that this case overruled Braunfeld v. Brown. The Court wrote quite narrowly, however, taking the position that employment without Saturday work was available in the community so that this particular Sabbatarian was genuinely in the labor market and thus was not being shown undue favoritism. Sherbert v. Verner, 374 U.S. 398 (1963).

There is no constitutional right to be a conscientious objector to military service. Conscientious objector statutes, however, cannot base status as a conscientious objector upon a belief in God or a "Supreme Being." Welsh v. United States, 398 U.S. 333 (1970). There is no constitutional right as part of a religious belief to claim the privilege to be a conscientious objector to certain wars as opposed to being a conscientious objector to all wars and all military activities. Gillette v. United States, 401 U.S. 437 (1971).

III. THE FEDERAL SYSTEM—
NATIONAL POWERS

1. The Nature of Federal Power

The federal government is a government of delegated powers. The federal government has no power unless a source for it is found in the Constitution. But where power has been granted, the federal power is supreme. The federal government has the power to create a United States bank under the "necessary and proper" clause of Article I, Section 8, of the Constitution. The "necessary and proper" clause constitutes a separate and additional grant of power to the national government beyond the other powers delegated in Article I, Section 8, of the Constitution, and a national bank is "appropriate" (necessary) to carry out those other delegated powers. McCulloch v. Maryland, 17 U.S. (4 Wheat.) 316 (1819).

In foreign law rather than internal domestic law, the federal government has inherent powers beyond those delegated to it because the United States is a nation in the family of nations and its organization on a federal basis is only an internal matter. United States v. Curtiss-Wright Export Corp., 299 U.S. 304 (1936).

2. The Federal Power Over Interstate and Foreign Commerce

The federal power over commerce extends to all matters which affect the states generally and to all matters with which it is necessary to deal for the purpose of effectively carrying out commerce powers. The power over interstate commerce extends to protecting interstate commerce within the boundaries of the various states. The federal government by licensing coast-wise shipping may authorize ships to enter the territorial waters of the states and ply their trade. Gibbons v. Ogden, 22 U. S. (9 Wheat.) 1 (1824).

The power to regulate interstate transportation includes the power to regulate intrastate transportation insofar as it affects interstate transportation. Intrastate transportation rates may have an effect upon interstate commerce because of competition between intrastate and interstate commodities. Houston, E. & W. Texas Ry. Co. v. United States, 234 U.S. 342 (1914).

Congress can prohibit the interstate transportation of goods produced for interstate commerce under substandard working conditions and can also regulate the production itself of goods destined for interstate commerce. United States v. Darby, 312 U.S. 100 (1941).

In a situation where the national government finds it necessary to ration and allocate the production of wheat or other agricultural commodity, it can ration and regulate the production of the commodity grown on a farm for consumption on that farm even though none of the commodity ever leaves that farm. Such homegrown agricultural products "overhang" the market, and if substantial amounts of them are put into the market, the regulation of the market is destroyed. Wickard v. Filburn, 317 U.S. 111 (1942).

Congress can prohibit racial discrimination in hotels and motels housing interstate travellers. Heart of Atlanta Motel v. United States, 379 U.S. 241 (1964).

Congress has the power to prohibit racial discrimination in restaurants even though there is no showing that any interstate travellers have used or intend to use the restaurant. There is sufficient connection with interstate commerce in showing that some of the food sold in the restaurant has moved in interstate commerce and some of the supplies used in the restaurant have done so. In this case, however, the Court failed to establish a clear nexus in its opinion showing an actual effect upon interstate commerce of racial discrimination in a restaurant which received food in interstate commerce since those persons discriminated against would still have to eat somewhere in the community. Katzenbach v. Mc-Clung, 379 U.S. 294 (1964). A more useful constitutional approach would have been to recognize that Congress can eliminate racial discrimination in all restaurants because permitting such discrimination has a serious impact upon the economic well-being of restaurants which cannot discriminate on a racial basis because they do serve interstate travellers.

The Court used the broader approach suggested in the preceding paragraph to justify regulation of "loan sharks" who engage in "extortionate credit transactions," even though there was no showing that the particular transactions had any relationship to interstate commerce. The Court said that Congress was engaged in the regulation of a "class of activities," some of which activities clearly affected interstate commerce. Perez v. United States, 402 U.S. 146 (1971).

3. The Taxing and Spending Power

Taxes can constitute a powerful regulatory device. But the use of taxes solely to accomplish regulation in a field where Congress otherwise does not have the power to regulate would thwart the principle limiting federal powers to delegated powers. A heavy federal tax on liquor dealers carrying on business in violation of state law coupled with a light tax on liquor dealers lawfully carrying on their business activities was found to be an unconstitutional regulation in United States v. Constantine, 296 U.S. 287 (1935).

Recognizing that many taxes have regulatory impact, however, the Court has usually upheld taxes which produce some revenue even though their major purpose would seem to be to accomplish a regulatory goal. A heavy tax upon sawed-off shotguns, machine guns, unusually small weapons which can be concealed on the person, and silencers was held constitutional as producing some revenue. Sonzinsky v. United States, 300 U.S. 506 (1937).

The power to spend money for the "general welfare" is an additional grant of power to the federal government and authorizes spending money for matters which fall within "general welfare" but which are not otherwise within delegated regulatory powers. United States v. Butler, 297 U.S. 1 (1936).

The retirement benefits under the Social Security Act, a program of taxation and the payment of benefits directly by the federal government, constitutes taxing and spending for the "general welfare" and is constitutional, even assuming that there is no regulatory power which would justify this federal program. Helvering v. Davis, 301 U. S. 619 (1937).

Federal financing of presidential election campaigns is spending for the "general welfare." Buckley v. Valeo, 424 U.S. 1 (1976).

4. War Powers

War powers can be exercised in peacetime to justify such federal programs as the building of a dam as part of the Tennessee Valley Authority complex because the electricity from the dam supplies power for the present or potential manufacture of nitrates and munitions. Ashwander v. Tennessee Valley Authority, 297 U.S. 288 (1936).

The federal government may continue to engage in rent control throughout the United States during peacetime as part of the power because of a housing deficit occasioned by war. Woods v. Cloyd W. Miller Co., 333 U.S. 138 (1948).

5. The Treaty Power

The treaty-making power of the federal government enables it to regulate within the United States where without a treaty there would be no delegated power upon which to base the regulation. A migratory bird treaty with Canada enabled the national government to regulate the protection and harvesting of migratory birds within the United States, even though it was assumed that without the treaty the federal government would not have the power. Missouri v. Holland, 252 U.S. 416 (1920).

Executive agreements are entitled to the same constitutional stature as treaties in the relationship between the states and the federal government. The supremacy clause makes both treaties and executive agreements supreme over state power as to the subjects covered by them. United States v. Belmont, 301 U.S. 324 (1937).

Treaties and executive agreements cannot limit or alter constitutional liberties. Executive agreements with our allies concerning the trial of criminal cases involving civilians who accompanied the military could not take away the constitutional right of civilians to have a jury trial in a civilian court in serious criminal cases. Reid v. Covert, 354 U.S. 1 (1957).

6. The Property Power

The property power authorizes the federal government to buy and sell property, including such property as the electric power produced by hydroelectric dams built under other federal powers. Ashwander v. Tennessee Valley Authority, 297 U.S. 288 (1936).

The federal property power extends to the protection of and regulations concerning wild horses on public lands under the Wild Free-Roaming Horses and Burros Act (1971). Kleppe v. New Mexico, 426 U.S. 529 (1976).

IV. STATE POWER TO REGULATE AND TAX WHICH OVERLAPS CONGRESSIONAL POWER

1. State Regulation, With Emphasis Upon Interstate Commerce

The grant of power to the federal government implies a prohibition against the state exercise of power at least in some situations. A grant of power to the federal government to create the United States Bank constituted an implied prohibition against a state regulating or taxing that bank. McCulloch v. Maryland, 17 U.S. (4 Wheat.) 316 (1819).

The Supreme Court, realizing that a similar analysis was necessary with respect to at least some aspects of the regulation of interstate commerce, carefully evaluated the implied prohibition analysis and almost accepted it, but then turned aside and merely found state regulation conflicting with federal regulation in the early leading case of Gibbons v. Ogden, 22 U.S. (9 Wheat.) 1 (1824).

The Court early recognized that it would be unwise to imply a constitutional prohibition against the states regulating interstate commerce in any way. The authorization by a state to build a dam across a creek which was part of a navigable river system was found constitutional by the Court as not interfering with the federal power over interstate commerce "in its dormant state." Willson v. Black Bird Creek Marsh Co., 27 U.S. (2 Pet.) 245 (1829).

The dilemma implicit in the need for an implied prohibition against the states regulating some aspects of interstate commerce but allowing them to regulate other aspects of interstate commerce was resolved by classifying interstate commerce as national and local. National commerce requires national uniformity of regulation and state regulations in this field constitute an undue burden on commerce. But local commerce does not require uniformity and can be diverse, and therefore the states can regulate in the local area until Congress stops them. Cooley v. Board of Wardens of the Port of Philadelphia, 53 U.S. (12 How.) 299 (1851).

As to all those matters where the states have the power to regulate in the commerce field because they are local in nature, the constitutional issue is simply whether the state regulation conflicts with congressional regulation. While this is a constitutional issue under the supremacy clause, it is resolved simply as an issue of whether federal and state statutes conflict. If conflict is found, the federal statute is supreme. A state statute prohibiting the operation on state highways of a motor vehicle carrying any other vehicle over the head of the operator of the carrier vehicle was held to be enforceable because it was not a regulation of "safety of operation and equipment" under the Federal Motor Carrier Act of 1935. Maurer v. Hamilton, 309 U.S. 598 (1940).

The federal regulatory scheme may be so complete that it is held to "occupy the field" and preempt any general state regulations in the same field, even though there is no precise statutory conflict. This is true with respect to the control of labor relations under the National Labor Relations Act. Guss v. Utah Labor Relations Board, 353 U.S. 1 (1957).

Under the "national interstate commerce" analysis, there is a broad area of interstate commerce where state regulations will be held to be unconstitutional even in the absence of a congressional regulatory policy. Here the Court recognizes an implied constitutional prohibition against the states regulating interstate commerce on the ground that state regulation would create an undue burden on commerce. Cooley v. Board of Wardens of the Port of Philadelphia, supra.

State regulations of interstate commerce will more likely be upheld if they involve safety and health considerations than if they involve an attempt to regulate economic competition. A refusal by a state to grant a permit to an interstate bus line on the ground that the particular route was adequately served was held unconstitutional in Buck v. Kuykendall, 267 U.S. 307 (1925). But a similar refusal to grant a permit because the particular highway was overcrowded with traffic was upheld in Bradley v. Public Utilities Commission, 289 U.S. 92 (1933).

State legislation limiting the length of freight and passenger trains was held to violate the implied prohibition of the commerce clause against the claim that it was a safety measure. The Court found that the safety aspects of the train-length limitation were weak and the burden on commerce, on balance, outweighed the state safety claim. Southern Pac. Co. v. Arizona, 325 U.S. 761 (1945).

Even those members of the Supreme Court who view with disfavor striking down state regulations passed for safety reasons concede that the implied prohibition analysis must be applied in some situations where safety is the claimed justification. A regulation by a state requiring a certain contoured mudguard on trucks and trailers contrary to the overwhleming requirements of the surrounding states, and which necessitated changing mudguards at the state line from the generally accepted ones, was held to constitute an undue burden on commerce and a violation of the implied prohibition of the commerce clause. Bibb v. Navajo Freight Lines, Inc., 359 U.S. 520 (1959).

States will be allowed to enforce genuine inspection laws and quarantines which protect against the spread of disease in livestock or agricultural products. Mintz v. Baldwin, 289 U.S. 346 (1933).

Inspection laws cannot be used, however, to set up economic barriers to free trade in commodities from state to state. Dean Milk Co. v. City of Madison, 340 U.S. 349 (1951). Nor can local price regulation justify state prohibition of the shipment of competing products at uncontrolled prices into the state. Baldwin v. G.A.F. Seelig, Inc., 294 U.S. 511 (1935).

A state may not attempt to satisfy local needs first by prohibiting the sale and interstate shipment out of a state of local products such as milk, H. P. Hood & Sons v. Du Mond, 336 U.S. 525 (1949), or even of natural resources such as natural gas, Pennsylvania v. West Virginia, 262 U.S. 553 (1923).

2. State Taxation, With Emphasis Upon Interstate Commerce

The Constitution cannot be taken as implying a prohibition against all state taxation of interstate commerce. This would give interstate commerce a strong competitive advantage over intrastate commerce. Interstate commerce must pay its own way. On the other hand, there is an implied constitutional prohibition against the states creating multiple tax burdens by levying taxes upon property or transactions which have also been taxed in other states. Equality of taxation between interstate and intrastate commerce is the goal. Henneford v. Silas Mason Co., 300 U.S. 577 (1937).

Equality is idealistic, and difficult to achieve in practice. The constitutional requirement for state taxation of interstate commerce is some sort of allocation formula which with reasonable accuracy reflects that portion of interstate commerce which can be attributed to a particular state. Although other formulas have been upheld, a standard three-factor formula is the best means of attributing the proper proportion of income from local aspects of interstate business. Such a formula compares the state portion of a business enterprise to the entire business enterprise with regard to these factors: (1) value of real and tangible personal property, (2) wages, salaries, commissions, and other compensation of employees, and (3) gross sales, less returns and allowances. Butler Bros. v. McColgan, 315 U.S. 501 (1942).

An ad valorem property tax upon moveable property which moves from state to state in an interstate business could not use a rigid mileage formula but had to approximate the value of the tangible assets permanently or habitually employed in the taxing state, including a portion of the intangible or "going-concern" value of the enterprise. Norfolk & Western Ry. Co. v. Missouri State Tax Comm., 390 U.S. 317 (1968).

A state was constitutionally authorized to tax the value of aircraft landing and taking off in the state, although the aircraft did not have their home bases in the state. The tax was upheld under an apportionment formula based upon the ratio of (1) aircraft arrivals and departures in the state as compared to throughout the airline system, (2) revenue tons handled by the airline at the airports in the state compared to throughout the airline system, and (3) originating revenues within the state as compared to throughout the system. Braniff Airways, Inc. v. Nebraska State Board of Equalization, 347 U.S. 590 (1954).

Goods imported into a state from interstate or foreign commerce became property located in the state so that ad valorem property taxes could be levied upon them. The goods had become commingled in the mass of property of the state by becoming a warehouse inventory held for local sale or order. Michelin Tire Corp. v. Wages, 423 U.S. 276 (1976).

Under an allocation formula, a state was allowed to levy a net income tax on sales made within the state although the only connection which the out-of-state company had with the state was a small sales office from which salesmen solicited orders which were sent directly outside the state for acceptance and direct shipment to the purchaser. Northwestern States Portland Cement Co. v. Minnesota, 358 U.S. 450 (1959). This holding resulted in the passage of 15 U.S.C. A. § 381 (1959) which forbids levying an income tax by any state if the only business activity of the company within the state is the solicitation of orders for the sale of tangible personal property, which orders are sent outside the state for approval, and, if approved, are filled by shipment or delivery from outside the state.

As a general rule, sales or gross receipts taxes cannot be levied on interstate transactions. However, use taxes, comparable in amount to sales taxes, can be levied in the state where the transaction is completed by the receipt of the goods for continued use in that state. By this means, interstate transactions carry the same tax burden as intrastate transactions and are not subject to multiple state taxation. Henneford v. Silas Mason Co., 300 U.S. 577 (1937).

A major problem is the collection of use taxes. If the company making the interstate sale had local sales offices or did business generally in the state where the transaction was completed and the use tax was levied, the company could be required to collect the use tax as part of the interstate transaction. General Trading Co. v. State Tax Comm., 322 U.S. 335 (1944). But if the transaction was accomplished solely by interstate communication, without local sales persons soliciting orders in the receiving state, the receiving state could not compel the collection of the use tax by the out-of-state company. National Bellas Hess, Inc. v. Dept. of Revenue, 386 U.S. 753 (1967).

Earlier cases held that any state tax which was couched in terms of granting a license or a franchise to do an interstate business was automatically unconstitutional whether or not it discriminated against interstate commerce by taxing more heavily than a similar intrastate license or franchise tax. It has now been held, however, that such taxes are to be tested in the same way as any other taxes solely to insure that interstate commerce is paying its own way but not paying more than intrastate commerce. The use of wording, such as license, franchise, or a tax upon the privilege to engage in business, does not control since liability for all taxes has the actual effect of conditioning the right to do business. Complete Auto Transit, Inc. v. Brady, 430 U.S. 274 (1977).

Some state taxes unquestionably put a heavier burden upon interstate commerce than upon intrastate commerce because of their nature, but they may, nevertheless, be upheld because of the importance of the local taxing incidence. This is particularly so of taxes levied by states upon the severance of natural resources, such as oil or coal, most of which resources will ultimately be shipped into interstate commerce. Oliver Iron Mining Co. v. Lord, 262 U.S. 172 (1923).

A small tax upon each commercial airline passenger using an airport, to help defray the costs of the airport construction, was held constitutional in Evansville–Vanderburgh Airport Authority Dist. v. Delta Airlines, 405 U.S. 707 (1972). This holding led to the enactment of 49 U.S.C.A. § 1513 which prohibits any such taxes levied on air travelers.

3. **Congressional Power to Consent to State Regulation and Taxation in Areas Otherwise Subject to an Implied Constitutional Prohibition**

The case which established the distinction between national and local interstate commerce, allowing the states to control local commerce but finding an implied prohibition against state control in national interstate commerce, said that Congress could not by statute give power to the states to control national interstate commerce which was subject to the implied constitutional prohibition against state control. Cooley v. Board of Wardens of the Port of Philadelphia, 53 U.S. (12 How.) 299 (1851).

In later years, however, the Court developed the doctrine that states could regulate in the field of national interstate commerce if Congress consented to such regulation. This doctrine includes the right of the state to prohibit interstate shipment into the state of certain commodities such as liquor, Clark Distilling Co. v. Western Maryland R. Co., 242 U.S. 311 (1917), and goods made by convict labor, Whitfield v. Ohio, 297 U.S. 431 (1936).

The one area where every member of the Court has always agreed that there is an implied constitutional prohibition against state regulation or taxation of interstate commerce has been in those instances where the state law discriminates against interstate commerce. Yet, the Court has held that Congress can consent even to state discrimination against interstate commerce. A state discriminatory tax against nonresident insurance companies was upheld, the Court recognizing the right of the state to favor local insurance companies in its tax program because of a congressional consent statute authorizing the states to regulate and tax the insurance business. Prudential Insurance Co. v. Benjamin, 328 U.S. 408 (1946).

The import of the decisions involving congressional consent is that the implied constitutional prohibition against state regulation and taxation in an unduly burdensome and discriminatory way includes the additional authorization to Congress to consent to such taxation and regulation. This is contrary to the *Cooley* case, supra, but has constitutional foundation. Note, for example, the second and third clauses of Article I, Section 10, of the Constitution which contain prohibitions against state regulation "without the Consent of Congress."

V. INTERGOVERNMENTAL IMMUNITIES

1. Taxation

There is an implied constitutional prohibition against a state taxing federal governmental instrumentalities. McCulloch v. Maryland, 17 U.S. (4 Wheat.) 316 (1819).

There is an implied constitutional prohibition against the federal government taxing instrumentalities of the states insofar as state governmental functions are involved. Collector v. Day, 78 U.S. (11 Wall.) 113 (1871). When a state engaged in a business enterprise which was of the same nature as enterprises commonly carried on by private interests, the state instrumentalities were not immune from federal taxation, as, for example, was the holding in a case involving bottled mineral waters. New York v. United States, 326 U.S. 572 (1946).

State income taxes on federal employees, and the federal income taxes on state employees were not considered to be taxing the governmental entity itself. Helvering v. Gerhardt, 304 U.S. 405 (1938); Graves v. New York ex rel. O'Keefe, 306 U.S. 466 (1939).

Taxes upon governmental property, state or federal, leased by and used by private business interests, were held constitutional. United States & Borg-Warner Corp. v. Detroit, 355 U.S. 466 (1958).

The federal government has frequently consented to state taxation of its instrumentalities. The constitutionality of this power to consent has never been specifically litigated, but the Supreme Court has recognized it. First Agricultural National Bank v. State Tax Comm., 392 U.S. 339 (1968). It is assumed also that a state could consent to federal taxation, although no instance of such consent has occurred.

2. Regulation

There is a constitutional prohibition against states regulating federal governmental activities and instrumentalities. These holdings are based upon the supremacy clause. In re Neagle, 135 U. S. 1 (1890).

For many years, it was held that the federal government had the power to regulate state government activities and instrumentalities under its delegated regulatory powers such as its power over interstate commerce. These were all cases, however, in which the federal government had not by its regulation attempted to penetrate deeply into state governmental activity. This earlier constitutional assumption was recently reversed. It was held unconstitutional to apply the federal wage and hour law to state employees generally because allowing such federal control took out of the hands of the state government the power to establish for its own employees its own employment policies and practices. National League of Cities v. Usery, 426 U.S. 833 (1976). This case engendered a great deal of controversy, but whether or not a sufficient burden upon state governmental functions was shown in this particular situation, the basic principle appears inescapably sound. For example, if the federal government applied the entire federal policy concerning collective bargaining, the right to strike, etc., contained in the National Labor Relations Act, to state employees, this would be an overwhelming interference with the right of the state to carry on its own business in the way it sees fit. Such a federal intrusion should be treated as beyond federal power.

It is assumed that states could consent to federal regulation of their instrumentalities. There are many instances where the federal government has consented to regulation of its instrumentalities by the states. The Federal Assimilative Crimes Act was held constitutional in authorizing the states to apply their criminal laws in federal enclaves located in the states. United States v. Sharpnack, 355 U.S. 286 (1958).

VI. THE RELATIONSHIPS BETWEEN AND AMONG THE STATES

Article I, Section 10, Clause 3, of the Constitution provides for the making of interstate compacts with the consent of Congress. By entering into such a compact, a state relinquishes its control over whether what it agrees to in the compact complies with its own internal constitution and laws. Once the compact is made, it is a legal document binding on the states, and its interpretation and application is a federal question. West Virginia v. Sims, 341 U.S. 22 (1951).

The Court has said the necessity of complying with the compact clause is limited to instances where the agreements are "directed to the formation of any combination tending to the increase of political power in the States, which may encroach upon or interfere with the just supremacy of the United States." Virginia v. Tennessee, 148 U.S. 503 (1893). So not all agreements between states fall under the interstate compact clause. States may contract with each other to buy and sell property or make agreements concerning road maintenance near state boundaries, etc. Even the settlement of a boundary dispute between states in the form of a consent judgment in the United States Supreme Court did not require the consent of Congress. New Hampshire v. Maine, 426 U.S. 363 (1976).

VII. RELATIONSHIPS AMONG THE BRANCHES OF THE FEDERAL GOVERNMENT

In setting up the Federal Election Commission, in 1974, Congress provided for the appointment of some of the members of the Commission by the President *pro tempore* of the Senate and the Speaker of the House. This provision for appointment of executive officials by the Houses of Congress was held to be a violation of the constitutional doctrine of separation of powers because the Constitution gives the appointing power to the Executive. Buckley v. Valeo, 424 U.S. 1 (1976).

President Nixon challenged the right of the United States District Court to subpoena recordings made of conversations between the President and others in the Oval Office in the White House. The Court recognized a presidential privilege against a general disclosure of confidential conversations which take place in the offices of the President. But the Court held the privilege was not absolute and unqualified. In the particular case the needs of the judicial process in enforcing the law where criminal conduct was suspected were held to outweigh presidential privilege. The Court upheld the right of the United States District Court to subpoena the tapes. United States v. Nixon, 418 U.S. 683 (1974). This decision on July 24, 1974, led directly to the resignation of President Nixon on August 9, 1974.

*

APPENDIX B

CONSTITUTION OF THE UNITED STATES OF AMERICA

WE THE PEOPLE of the United States, in Order to form a more perfect Union, establish Justice, insure domestic Tranquility, provide for the common defence, promote the general Welfare, and secure the Blessings of Liberty to ourselves and our posterity, do ordain and establish this Constitution for the United States of America.

ARTICLE I.

SECTION 1. All legislative Powers herein granted shall be vested in a Congress of the United States, which shall consist of a Senate and House of Representatives.

SECTION 2. The House of Representatives shall be composed of Members chosen every second Year by the People of the several States, and the Electors in each State shall have the Qualifications requisite for Electors of the most numerous Branch of the State Legislature.

No person shall be a Representative who shall not have attained to the Age of twenty five Years, and been seven Years a Citizen of the United States, and who shall not, when elected, be an Inhabitant of that State in which he shall be chosen.

[*339*]

Representatives and direct Taxes shall be apportioned among the several States which may be included within this Union, according to their respective Numbers, which shall be determined by adding to the whole Number of free Persons, including those bound to Service for a Term of Years, and excluding Indians not taxed, three fifths of all other Persons. The actual Enumeration shall be made within three Years after the first Meeting of the Congress of the United States, and within every subsequent Term of ten Years, in such Manner as they shall by Law direct. The Number of Representatives shall not exceed one for every thirty Thousand, but each State shall have at Least one Representative; and until such enumeration shall be made, the State of New Hampshire shall be entitled to chuse three, Massachusetts eight, Rhode-Island and Providence Plantations one, Connecticut five, New-York six, New Jersey four, Pennsylvania eight, Delaware one, Maryland six, Virginia ten, North Carolina five, South Carolina five, and Georgia three.

When vacancies happen in the Representation from any State, the Executive Authority thereof shall issue Writs of Election to fill such Vacancies.

The House of Representatives shall chuse their Speaker and other Officers; and shall have the sole Power of Impeachment.

SECTION 3. The Senate of the United States shall be composed of two Senators from each State, chosen by the Legislature thereof, for six Years; and each Senator shall have one Vote.

Immediately after they shall be assembled in Consequence of the first Election, they shall be divided as equally as may be into three Classes. The Seats of the Senators of the first Class shall be vacated at the Expiration of the second year, of the second Class at the Expiration of the fourth Year, and of the third Class at the Expiration of the sixth Year, so that one third may be chosen every second Year; and if Vacancies happen by Resignation, or otherwise, during the Recess of the Legislature of any State, the Executive thereof may make temporary Appointments until the next Meeting of the Legislature, which shall then fill such Vacancies.

No Person shall be a Senator who shall not have attained to the Age of thirty Years, and been nine Years a Citizen of the United States, and who shall not, when elected, be an Inhabitant of that State for which he shall be chosen.

The Vice President of the United States shall be President of the Senate, but shall have no Vote, unless they be equally divided.

The Senate shall chuse their other Officers, and also a President pro tempore, in the Absence of the Vice President, or when he shall exercise the Office of President of the United States.

The Senate shall have the sole Power to try all Impeachments. When sitting for that Purpose, they shall be on Oath or Affirmation. When the President of the United States is tried, the Chief Justice shall preside: And no Person shall be convicted without the Concurrence of two thirds of the Members present.

Judgment in Cases of Impeachment shall not extend further than to removal from Office, and disqualification to hold and enjoy any Office of honor, Trust or Profit under the United States: but the Party convicted shall nevertheless be liable and subject to Indictment, Trial, Judgment and Punishment, according to Law.

SECTION 4. The Times, Places and Manner of holding Elections for Senators and Representatives, shall be prescribed in each State by the Legislature thereof; but the Congress may at any time by Law make or alter such Regulations, except as to the Places of chusing Senators.

The Congress shall assemble at least once in every Year, and such Meeting shall be on the first Monday in December, unless they shall by Law appoint a different Day.

SECTION 5. Each House shall be the Judge of the Elections, Returns and Qualifications of its own Members, and a Majority of each shall constitute a Quorum to do Business; but a smaller Number may adjourn from day to day, and may be authorized to compel the Attendance of absent Members, in such Manner, and under such Penalties as each House may provide.

Each House may determine the Rules of its Proceedings, punish its Members for disorderly Behaviour, and, with the Concurrence of two thirds, expel a Member.

Each House shall keep a Journal of its Proceedings, and from time to time publish the same, excepting such Parts as may in their Judgment require Secrecy; and the Yeas and Nays of the Members of either House on any question shall, at the Desire of one fifth of those present, be entered on the Journal.

Neither House, during the Session of Congress, shall, without the Consent of the other, adjourn for more than three days, nor to any other Place than that in which the two Houses shall be sitting.

SECTION 6. The Senators and Representatives shall receive a Compensation for their Services, to be ascertained by Law, and paid out of the Treasury of the United States. They shall in all Cases, except Treason, Felony and Breach of the Peace, be privileged from Arrest during their Attendance at the Session of their respective Houses, and in going to and returning from the same; and for any Speech or Debate in either House, they shall not be questioned in any other Place.

No Senator or Representative shall, during the Time for which he was elected, be appointed to any civil Office under the Authority of the United States, which shall have been created, or the Emoluments whereof shall have been encreased during such time; and no Person holding any Office under the United States, shall be a Member of either House during his Continuance in Office.

SECTION 7. All Bills for raising Revenue shall originate in the House of Representatives; but the Senate may propose or concur with Amendments as on other Bills.

Every Bill which shall have passed the House of Representatives and the Senate, shall, before it become a Law, be presented to the President of the United States; If he approves he shall sign it, but if not he shall return it, with his Objections to that House in which it shall have originated, who shall enter the Objections at large on their Journal, and proceed to reconsider it. If after such Reconsideration two thirds of that House shall agree to pass the Bill, it shall be sent, together with the Objections, to the other House, by which it shall likewise be reconsidered, and if approved by two thirds of that House, it shall become a Law. But in all such Cases the Votes of both Houses shall be determined by Yeas and Nays, and the Names of the Persons voting for and against the Bill shall be entered on the Journal of each House respectively. If any Bill shall not be returned by the President within ten Days (Sundays excepted) after it shall have been presented to him, the Same shall be a Law, in like Manner as if he had signed it, unless the Congress by their Adjournment prevent its Return, in which Case it shall not be a Law.

Every Order, Resolution, or Vote to which the Concurrence of the Senate and House of Representatives may be necessary (except on a question of Adjournment) shall be presented to the President of the United States; and before the Same shall take Effect, shall be approved by him, or being disapproved by him, shall be repassed by two thirds of the Senate and House of Representatives, according to the Rules and Limitations prescribed in the Case of a Bill.

SECTION 8. The Congress shall have Power To lay and collect Taxes, Duties, Imposts and Excises, to pay the Debts and provide for the common Defence and general Welfare of the United States; but all Duties, Imposts and Excises shall be uniform throughout the United States;

To borrow Money on the credit of the United States;

To regulate Commerce with foreign Nations, and among the several States, and with the Indian Tribes;

To establish a uniform Rule of Naturalization, and uniform Laws on the subject of Bankruptcies throughout the United States;

To coin Money, regulate the Value thereof, and of foreign Coin, and fix the Standard of Weights and Measures;

To provide for the Punishment of counterfeiting the Securities and current Coin of the United States;

To establish Post Offices and post Roads;

To promote the Progress of Science and useful Arts, by securing for limited Times to Authors and Inventors the exclusive Right to their respective Writings and Discoveries;

To constitute Tribunals inferior to the supreme Court;

To define and punish Piracies and Felonies committed on the high Seas, and Offences against the Law of Nations;

To declare War, grant Letters of Marque and Reprisal, and make Rules concerning Captures on Land and Water;

To raise and support Armies, but no Appropriation of Money to that Use shall be for a longer Term than two Years;

To provide and maintain a Navy;

To make Rules for the Government and Regulation of the land and naval Forces;

To provide for calling forth the Militia to execute the Laws of the Union, suppress Insurrections and repel Invasions;

To provide for organizing, arming, and disciplining, the Militia, and for governing such Part of them as may be employed in the Service of the United States, reserving to the States respectively, the Appointment of the Officers, and the Authority of training the Militia according to the discipline prescribed by Congress;

To exercise exclusive Legislation in all Cases whatsoever, over such District (not exceeding ten Miles square) as may, by Cession of particular States, and the Acceptance of Congress, become the Seat of the Government of the United States, and to exercise like Authority over all Places purchased by the Consent of the Legislature of the State in which the Same shall be, for the Erection of Forts, Magazines, Arsenals, dock-Yards, and other needful Buildings;—And

To make all Laws which shall be necessary and proper for carrying into Execution the foregoing

Powers, and all other Powers vested by this Constitution in the Government of the United States, or in any Department or Officer thereof.

SECTION 9. The Migration or Importation of such Persons as any of the States now existing shall think proper to admit, shall not be prohibited by the Congress prior to the Year one thousand eight hundred and eight, but a Tax or duty may be imposed on such Importation, not exceeding ten dollars for each Person.

The Privilege of the Writ of Habeas Corpus shall not be suspended, unless when in Cases of Rebellion or Invasion the public Safety may require it.

No Bill of Attainder or ex post facto Law shall be passed.

No Capitation, or other direct, Tax shall be laid, unless in Proportion to the Census or Enumeration herein before directed to be taken.

No Tax or Duty shall be laid on Articles exported from any State.

No Preference shall be given by any Regulation of Commerce or Revenue to the Ports of one State over those of another: nor shall Vessels bound to, or from, one State, be obliged to enter, clear, or pay Duties in another.

No Money shall be drawn from the Treasury, but in Consequence of Appropriations made by

Law; and a regular Statement and Account of the Receipts and Expenditures of all public Money shall be published from time to time.

No Title of Nobility shall be granted by the United States: And no Person holding any Office of Profit or Trust under them, shall, without the Consent of the Congress, accept of any present Emolument, Office, or Title, of any kind whatever, from any King, Prince, or foreign State.

SECTION 10. No State shall enter into any Treaty, Alliance, or Confederation; grant Letters of Marque and Reprisal; coin Money; emit Bills of Credit; make any Thing but gold and silver Coin a Tender in Payment of Debts; pass any Bill of Attainder, ex post facto Law, or Law impairing the Obligation of Contracts, or grant any Title of Nobility.

No State shall, without the Consent of the Congress, lay any Imposts or Duties on Imports or Exports, except what may be absolutely necessary for executing it's inspection Laws: and the net Produce of all Duties and Imposts, laid by any State on Imports or Exports, shall be for the Use of the Treasury of the United States; and all such Laws shall be subject to the Revision and Controul of the Congress.

No State shall, without the Consent of Congress, lay any Duty of Tonnage, keep Troops, or

Ships of War in time of Peace, enter into any Agreement or Compact with another State, or with a foreign Power, or engage in War, unless actually invaded, or in such imminent Danger as will not admit of delay.

ARTICLE II.

SECTION 1.   The executive Power shall be vested in a President of the United States of America. He shall hold his Office during the Term of four Years, and, together with the Vice President, chosen for the Same Term, be elected, as follows

Each State shall appoint, in such Manner as the Legislature thereof may direct, a Number of Electors, equal to the whole Number of Senators and Representatives to which the State may be entitled in the Congress: but no Senator or Representative, or Person holding an Office of Trust or Profit under the United States, shall be appointed an Elector.

The Electors shall meet in their respective States, and vote by Ballot for two Persons of whom one at least shall not be an Inhabitant of the same State with themselves.   And they shall make a List of all the Persons voted for, and of the Number of Votes for each; which List they shall sign and certify, and transmit sealed to the Seat of the Government of the United States, directed to the President of the Senate.   The President of the

Senate shall, in the Presence of the Senate and House of Representatives, open all the Certificates, and the Votes shall then be counted. The Person having the greatest Number of Votes shall be the President, if such Number be a Majority of the whole Number of Electors appointed; and if there be more than one who have such Majority, and have an equal Number of Votes, then the House of Representatives shall immediately chuse by Ballot one of them for President; and if no Person have a Majority, then from the five highest on the List the said House shall in like Manner chuse the President. But in chusing the President, the Votes shall be taken by States, the Representation from each State having one Vote; A quorum for this Purpose shall consist of a Member or Members from two thirds of the States, and a Majority of all the States shall be necessary to a Choice. In every Case, after the Choice of the President, the Person having the greatest Number of Votes of the Electors shall be the Vice President. But if there should remain two or more who have equal Votes, the Senate shall chuse from them by Ballot the Vice President.

The Congress may determine the Time of chusing the Electors, and the Day on which they shall give their Votes; which Day shall be the same throughout the United States.

No Person except a natural born Citizen, or a Citizen of the United States, at the time of the Adoption of this Constitution, shall be eligible to the Office of President; neither shall any Person be eligible to that Office who shall not have attained to the Age of thirty five Years, and been fourteen Years a Resident within the United States.

In Case of the Removal of the President from Office, or of his Death, Resignation, or Inability to discharge the Powers and Duties of the said Office, the same shall devolve on the Vice President, and the Congress may by Law provide for the Case of Removal, Death, Resignation or Inability, both of the President and Vice President, declaring what Officer shall then act as President, and such Officer shall act accordingly, until the Disability be removed, or a President shall be elected.

The President shall, at stated Times, receive for his Services, a Compensation, which shall neither be encreased nor diminished during the Period for which he shall have been elected, and he shall not receive within that Period any other Emolument from the United States, or any of them.

Before he enter on the Execution of his Office, he shall take the following Oath or Affirmation:— "I do solemnly swear (or affirm) that I will faithfully execute the Office of President of the United

States, and will to the best of my Ability, preserve, protect and defend the Constitution of the United States."

SECTION 2. The President shall be Commander in Chief of the Army and Navy of the United States, and of the Militia of the several States, when called into the actual Service of the United States; he may require the Opinion, in writing, of the principal Officer in each of the executive Departments, upon any Subject relating to the Duties of their respective Offices, and he shall have Power to grant Reprieves and Pardons for Offences against the United States, except in Cases of Impeachment.

He shall have Power, by and with the Advice and Consent of the Senate, to make Treaties, provided two thirds of the Senators present concur; and he shall nominate, and by and with the Advice and Consent of the Senate, shall appoint Ambassadors, other public Ministers and Consuls, Judges of the supreme Court, and all other Officers of the United States, whose Appointments are not herein otherwise provided for, and which shall be established by Law: but the Congress may by Law vest the Appointment of such inferior Officers, as they think proper, in the President alone, in the Courts of Law, or in the Heads of Departments.

The President shall have Power to fill up all Vacancies that may happen during the Recess of the Senate, by granting Commissions which shall expire at the End of their next Session.

SECTION 3. He shall from time to time give to the Congress Information of the State of the Union, and recommend to their Consideration such Measures as he shall judge necessary and expedient; he may, on extraordinary Occasions, convene both Houses, or either of them, and in Case of Disagreement between them, with Respect to the Time of Adjournment, he may adjourn them to such Time as he shall think proper; he shall receive Ambassadors and other public Ministers; he shall take Care that the Laws be faithfully executed, and shall Commission all the Officers of the United States.

SECTION 4. The President, Vice President and all civil Officers of the United States, shall be removed from Office on Impeachment for, and Conviction of, Treason, Bribery, or other high Crimes and Misdemeanors.

ARTICLE III.

SECTION 1. The judicial Power of the United States, shall be vested in one supreme Court, and in such inferior Courts as the Congress may from time to time ordain and establish. The Judges, both of the supreme and inferior Courts, shall hold their Offices during good Behaviour, and shall, at stated Times, receive for their Services, a Compensation, which shall not be diminished during their Continuance in Office.

SECTION 2. The judicial Power shall extend to all Cases, in Law and Equity, arising under this Constitution, the Laws of the United States, and Treaties made, or which shall be made, under their Authority;—to all Cases affecting Ambassadors, other public Ministers and Consuls;—to all Cases of admiralty and maritime Jurisdiction;—to Controversies to which the United States shall be a Party;—to Controversies between two or more States;—between a State and Citizens of another State;—between Citizens of different States,— between Citizens of the same State claiming Lands under Grants of different States, and between a State, or the Citizens thereof, and foreign States, Citizens or Subjects.

In all Cases affecting Ambassadors, other public Ministers and Consuls, and those in which a State shall be Party, the supreme Court shall have original Jurisdiction. In all the other Cases before mentioned, the supreme Court shall have appellate Jurisdiction, both as to Law and Fact, with such Exceptions, and under such Regulations as the Congress shall make.

The Trial of all Crimes, except in Cases of Impeachment, shall be by Jury; and such Trial shall be held in the State where the said Crimes shall have been committed; but when not committed within any State, the Trial shall be at such Place or Places as the Congress may by Law have directed.

Section 3. Treason against the United States, shall consist only in levying War against them, or in adhering to their Enemies, giving them Aid and Comfort. No Person shall be convicted of Treason unless on the Testimony of two Witnesses to the same overt Act, or on Confession in open Court.

The Congress shall have Power to declare the Punishment of Treason, but no Attainder of Treason shall work Corruption of Blood, or Forfeiture except during the Life of the Person attainted.

Article IV.

Section 1. Full Faith and Credit shall be given in each State to the public Acts, Records, and judicial Proceedings of every other State. And the Congress may by general Laws prescribe the Manner in which such Acts, Records and Proceedings shall be proved, and the Effect thereof.

Section 2. The Citizens of each State shall be entitled to all Privileges and Immunities of Citizens in the several States.

A Person charged in any State with Treason, Felony, or other Crime, who shall flee from Justice, and be found in another State, shall on Demand of the executive Authority of the State from which he fled, be delivered up, to be removed to the State having Jurisdiction of the Crime.

No Person held to Service or Labour in one State, under the Laws thereof, escaping into another, shall, in Consequence of any Law or Regulation therein, be discharged from such Service or Labour, but shall be delivered up on Claim of the Party to whom such Service or Labour may be due.

SECTION 3. New States may be admitted by the Congress into this Union; but no new State shall be formed or erected within the Jurisdiction of any other State; nor any State be formed by the Junction of two or more States, or Parts of States, without the Consent of the Legislatures of the States concerned as well as of the Congress.

The Congress shall have Power to dispose of and make all needful Rules and Regulations respecting the Territory or other Property belonging to the United States; and nothing in this Constitution shall be so construed as to Prejudice any Claims of the United States, or of any particular State.

SECTION 4. The United States shall guarantee to every State in this Union a Republican Form of

Government, and shall protect each of them against Invasion; and on Application of the Legislature, or of the Executive (when the Legislature cannot be convened) against domestic Violence.

ARTICLE V.

The Congress, whenever two thirds of both Houses shall deem it necessary, shall propose Amendments to this Constitution, or on the Application of the Legislatures of two thirds of the several States, shall call a Convention for proposing Amendments, which, in either Case, shall be valid to all Intents and Purposes, as Part of this Constitution, when ratified by the Legislatures of three fourths of the several States, or by Conventions in three fourths thereof, as the one or the other Mode of Ratification may be proposed by the Congress; Provided that no Amendment which may be made prior to the Year One thousand eight hundred and eight shall in any Manner affect the first and fourth Clauses in the Ninth Section of the first Article; and that no State, without its Consent, shall be deprived of its equal Suffrage in the Senate.

ARTICLE VI.

All Debts contracted and Engagements entered into, before the Adoption of this Constitution, shall be as valid against the United States under this Constitution, as under the Confederation.

This Constitution, and the laws of the United States which shall be made in Pursuance thereof; and all Treaties made, or which shall be made, under the Authority of the United States, shall be the supreme Law of the Land; and the Judges in every State shall be bound thereby, any Thing in the Constitution or Laws of any State to the Contrary notwithstanding.

The Senators and Representatives before mentioned, and the Members of the several State Legislatures, and all executive and judicial Officers, both of the United States and of the several States, shall be bound by Oath or Affirmation, to support this Constitution; but no religious Test shall ever be required as a Qualification to any Office or public Trust under the United States.

ARTICLE VII.

The Ratification of the Conventions of nine States, shall be sufficient for the Establishment of this Constitution between the States so ratifying the Same.

ARTICLES IN ADDITION TO, AND AMENDMENT OF THE CONSTITUTION OF THE UNITED STATES OF AMERICA, PROPOSED BY CONGRESS, AND RATIFIED BY THE LEGISLATURES OF THE SEVERAL STATES, PURSUANT TO THE

FIFTH ARTICLE OF THE ORIGINAL CONSTITUTION.

AMENDMENT I
[1791]

Congress shall make no law respecting an establishment of religion, or prohibiting the free exercise thereof; or abridging the freedom of speech, or of the press; or the right of the people peaceably to assemble, and to petition the Government for a redress of grievances.

AMENDMENT II
[1791]

A well regulated militia, being necessary to the security of a free State, the right of the people to keep and bear arms, shall not be infringed.

AMENDMENT III
[1791]

No Soldier shall, in time of peace be quartered in any house, without the consent of the owner, nor in time of war, but in a manner to be prescribed by law.

AMENDMENT IV
[1791]

The right of the people to be secure in their persons, houses, papers, and effects, against unreasonable searches and seizures, shall not be violated, and no warrants shall issue, but upon probable cause, supported by oath or affirmation, and particularly describing the place to be searched, and the persons or things to be seized.

AMENDMENT V
[1791]

No person shall be held to answer for a capital, or otherwise infamous crime, unless on a presentment or indictment of a Grand Jury, except in cases arising in the land or naval forces, or in the militia, when in actual service in time of war or public danger; nor shall any person be subject for the same offence to be twice put in jeopardy of life or limb; nor shall be compelled in any criminal case to be a witness against himself, nor be deprived of life, liberty, or property, without due process of law; nor shall private property be taken for public use, without just compensation.

AMENDMENT VI
[1791]

In all criminal prosecutions, the accused shall enjoy the right to a speedy and public trial, by an impartial jury of the State and district wherein the crime shall have been committed, which district shall have been previously ascertained by law, and to be informed of the nature and cause of the accusation; to be confronted with the witnesses against him; to have compulsory process for obtaining witnesses in his favor, and to have the assistance of counsel for his defence.

Amendment VII
[1791]

In Suits at common law, where the value in controversy shall exceed twenty dollars, the right of trial by jury shall be preserved, and no fact tried by a jury, shall be otherwise reexamined in any Court of the United States, than according to the rules of the common law.

Amendment VIII
[1791]

Excessive bail shall not be required, nor excessive fines imposed, nor cruel and unusual punishments inflicted.

Amendment IX
[1791]

The enumeration in the Constitution, of certain rights, shall not be construed to deny or disparage others retained by the people.

Amendment X
[1791]

The powers not delegated to the United States by the Constitution, nor prohibited by it to the

States, are reserved to the States respectively, or to the people.

AMENDMENT XI
[1798]

The Judicial power of the United States shall not be construed to extend to any suit in law or equity, commenced or prosecuted against one of the United States by Citizens of another State, or by Citizens or Subjects of any Foreign State.

AMENDMENT XII
[1804]

The Electors shall meet in their respective states, and vote by ballot for President and Vice-President, one of whom, at least, shall not be an inhabitant of the same state with themselves; they shall name in their ballots the person voted for as President, and in distinct ballots the person voted for as Vice-President, and they shall make distinct lists of all persons voted for as President, and of all persons voted for as Vice-President, and of the number of votes for each, which lists they shall sign and certify, and transmit sealed to the seat of the government of the United States, directed to the President of the Senate;— The President of the Senate shall, in the presence of the Senate and House of Representatives, open all the certificates and the votes shall then be counted;—The person having the greatest number of votes for President, shall be the President, if such number be a majority of the whole number of Electors appointed; and if no person have such majority, then from the persons having the highest numbers not exceeding three on the list of those voted for as President, the House of Representatives shall choose immediately, by ballot, the President. But in choosing the President, the votes shall be taken by states, the representation from each state having one vote; a quorum for this purpose shall consist of a member or members from two-thirds of the states, and a majority of all the states shall be necessary to a choice. And if the House of Representatives shall not choose a President whenever the right of choice shall devolve upon them, before the fourth day of March next following, then the Vice-President shall act as President, as in the case of the death or other constitutional disability of the President.—The person having the greatest number of votes as Vice-President, shall be the Vice-President, if such number be a majority of the whole number of Electors appointed, and if no person have a majority, then from the two highest numbers on the list, the Senate shall choose the Vice-President; a quorum for the purpose shall consist of two-thirds of the whole number of Senators, and a majority of the whole number shall be necessary to a choice. But no person constitutionally ineligible to the office of President shall be eligible to that of Vice-President of the United States.

AMENDMENT XIII
[1865]

SECTION 1. Neither slavery nor involuntary servitude, except as a punishment for crime whereof the party shall have been duly convicted, shall exist within the United States, or any place subject to their jurisdiction.

SECTION 2. Congress shall have power to enforce this article by appropriate legislation.

AMENDMENT XIV
[1868]

SECTION 1. All persons born or naturalized in the United States, and subject to the jurisdiction thereof, are citizens of the United States and of the State wherein they reside. No State shall make or enforce any law which shall abridge the privileges or immunities of citizens of the United States; nor shall any State deprive any person of life, liberty, or property, without due process of law; nor deny to any person within its jurisdiction the equal protection of the laws.

SECTION 2. Representatives shall be apportioned among the several States according to their respective numbers, counting the whole number of persons in each State, excluding Indians not taxed. But when the right to vote at any election for the choice of electors for President and Vice President of the United States, Representatives in Congress, the Executive and Judicial officers of a State, or the members of the Legislature thereof, is denied to any of the male inhabitants of such State, being twenty-one years of age, and citizens of the United States, or in any way abridged, except for participation in rebellion, or other crime, the basis of representation therein shall be reduced in the proportion which the number of such male citizens shall bear to the whole number of male citizens twenty-one years of age in such State.

SECTION 3. No person shall be a Senator or Representative in Congress, or elector of President and Vice President, or hold any office, civil or military, under the United States, or under any State, who, having previously taken an oath, as a member of Congress, or as an officer of the United States, or as a member of any State legislature, or as an executive or judicial officer of any State, to support the Constitution of the United States, shall have engaged in insurrection or rebellion against the same, or given aid or comfort to the enemies thereof. But Congress may by a vote of two-thirds of each House, remove such disability.

SECTION 4. The validity of the public debt of the United States, authorized by law, including debts incurred for payment of pensions and bounties for services in suppressing insurrection or rebellion, shall not be questioned. But neither the United States nor any State shall assume or pay any debt or obligation incurred in aid of insurrection or rebellion against the United States, or any claim for the loss or emancipation of any slave; but all such debts, obligations and claims shall be held illegal and void.

SECTION 5. The Congress shall have power to enforce, by appropriate legislation, the provisions of this article.

AMENDMENT XV
[1870]

SECTION 1. The right of citizens of the United States to vote shall not be denied or abridged by the United States or by any State on account of race, color, or previous condition of servitude.

SECTION 2. The Congress shall have power to enforce this article by appropriate legislation.

AMENDMENT XVI
[1913]

The Congress shall have power to lay and collect taxes on incomes, from whatever source derived, without apportionment among the several States, and without regard to any census or enumeration.

AMENDMENT XVII
[1913]

The Senate of the United States shall be composed of two Senators from each State, elected by the people thereof, for six years; and each Senator shall have one vote. The electors in each State shall have the qualifications requisite for electors of the most numerous branch of the State legislatures.

When vacancies happen in the representation of any State in the Senate, the executive authority of such State shall issue writs of election to fill such vacancies: *Provided,* That the legislature of any State may empower the executive thereof to make temporary appointments until the people fill the vacancies by election as the legislature may direct.

This amendment shall not be so construed as to affect the election or term of any Senator chosen before it becomes valid as part of the Constitution.

AMENDMENT XVIII
[1919]

SECTION 1. After one year from the ratification of this article the manufacture, sale, or transportation of intoxicating liquors within, the importation thereof into, or the exportation thereof from the United States and all territory subject to the jurisdiction thereof for beverage purposes is hereby prohibited.

SECTION 2. The Congress and the several States shall have concurrent power to enforce this article by appropriate legislation.

SECTION 3. This article shall be inoperative unless it shall have been ratified as an amendment to the Constitution by the legislatures of the several States, as provided in the Constitution, within seven years from the date of the submission hereof to the States by the Congress.

AMENDMENT XIX
[1920]

The right of citizens of the United States to vote shall not be denied or abridged by the United States or by any State on account of sex.

Congress shall have power to enforce this article by appropriate legislation.

AMENDMENT XX
[1933]

SECTION 1. The terms of the President and Vice President shall end at noon on the 20th day of January, and the terms of Senators and Representatives at noon on the 3d day of January, of the years in which such terms would have ended if this article had not been ratified; and the terms of their successors shall then begin.

SECTION 2. The Congress shall assemble at least once in every year, and such meeting shall begin at noon on the 3d day of January, unless they shall by law appoint a different day.

SECTION 3. If, at the time fixed for the beginning of the term of the President, the President elect shall have died, the Vice President elect shall become President. If a President shall not have been chosen before the time fixed for the beginning of his term, or if the President elect shall have failed to qualify, then the Vice President elect shall act as President until a President shall have qualified; and the Congress may by law provide for the case wherein neither a President elect nor a Vice President elect shall have qualified, declaring who shall then act as President, or the manner in which one who is to act shall be selected, and such person shall act accordingly until a President or Vice President shall have qualified.

SECTION 4. The Congress may by law provide for the case of the death of any of the persons from whom the House of Representatives may choose a President whenever the rights of choice shall have devolved upon them, and for the case of the death of any of the persons from whom the Senate may choose a Vice President whenever the right of choice shall have devolved upon them.

SECTION 5. Sections 1 and 2 shall take effect on the 15th day of October following the ratification of this article.

SECTION 6. This article shall be inoperative unless it shall have been ratified as an amendment to the Constitution by the legislatures of three-fourths of the several States within seven years from the date of its submission.

AMENDMENT XXI
[1933]

SECTION 1. The eighteenth article of amendment to the Constitution of the United States is hereby repealed.

SECTION 2. The transportation or importation into any State, Territory, or possession of the United States for delivery or use therein of intoxicating liquors, in violation of the laws thereof, is hereby prohibited.

SECTION 3. This article shall be inoperative unless it shall have been ratified as an amendment to the Constitution by conventions in the several States, as provided in the Constitution, within seven years from the date of the submission hereof to the States by the Congress.

AMENDMENT XXII
[1951]

SECTION 1. No person shall be elected to the office of the President more than twice, and no person who has held the office of President, or acted as President, for more than two years of a term to which some other person was elected President shall be elected to the office of the President more than once. But this Article shall not apply to any person holding the office of President when this Article was proposed by the Congress, and shall not prevent any person who may be holding the office of President, or acting as President, during the term within which this Article becomes operative from holding the office of President or acting as President during the remainder of such term.

SECTION 2. This article shall be inoperative unless it shall have been ratified as an amendment to the Constitution by the legislatures of three-fourths of the several States within seven years from the date of its submission to the States by the Congress.

AMENDMENT XXIII
[1961]

SECTION 1. The District constituting the seat of Government of the United States shall appoint in such manner as the Congress may direct:

A number of electors of President and Vice President equal to the whole number of Senators and Representatives in Congress to which the District would be entitled if it were a State, but in no event more than the least populous State; they shall be in addition to those appointed by the

States, but they shall be considered, for the purposes of the election of President and Vice President, to be electors appointed by a State; and they shall meet in the District and perform such duties as provided by the twelfth article of amendment.

SECTION 2. The Congress shall have power to enforce this article by appropriate legislation.

AMENDMENT XXIV
[1964]

SECTION 1. The right of citizens of the United States to vote in any primary or other election for President or Vice President, for electors for President or Vice President, or for Senator or Representative in Congress, shall not be denied or abridged by the United States or any State by reason of failure to pay any poll tax or other tax.

SECTION 2. The Congress shall have power to enforce this article by appropriate legislation.

AMENDMENT XXV
[1967]

SECTION 1. In case of the removal of the President from office or of his death or resignation, the Vice President shall become President.

SECTION 2. Whenever there is a vacancy in the office of the Vice President, the President shall nominate a Vice President who shall take office upon confirmation by a majority vote of both Houses of Congress.

Section 3. Whenever the President transmits to the President pro tempore of the Senate and the Speaker of the House of Representatives his written declaration that he is unable to discharge the powers and duties of his office, and until he transmits to them a written declaration to the contrary, such powers and duties shall be discharged by the Vice President as Acting President.

Section 4. Whenever the Vice President and a majority of either the principal officers of the executive departments or of such other body as Congress may by law provide, transmit to the President pro tempore of the Senate and the Speaker of the House of Representatives their written declaration that the President is unable to discharge the powers and duties of his office, the Vice President shall immediately assume the powers and duties of the office as Acting President.

Thereafter, when the President transmits to the President pro tempore of the Senate and the Speaker of the House of Representatives his written declaration that no inability exists, he shall resume the powers and duties of his office unless the Vice President and a majority of either the principal officers of the executive department or of such other body as Congress may by law provide, transmit within four days to the President pro tempore of the Senate and the Speaker of the House of Representatives their written declaration that the President is unable to discharge the powers and duties of his office. Thereupon Congress shall decide the issue, assembling within forty-eight hours for that purpose if not in session. If the Congress, within twenty-one days after receipt of the latter written declaration, or, if Congress is not in session, within twenty-one days after Congress is required to assemble, determines by two-thirds vote of both Houses that the President is unable to discharge the powers and duties of his office, the Vice President shall continue to discharge the same as Acting President; otherwise, the President shall resume the powers and duties of his office.

AMENDMENT XXVI
[1971]

SECTION 1. The right of citizens of the United States, who are eighteen years of age or older, to vote shall not be denied or abridged by the United States or by any State on account of age.

SECTION 2. The Congress shall have power to enforce this article by appropriate legislation.

APPENDIX B

AMENDMENT XXVII
[Proposed]

SECTION 1. Equality of rights under the law shall not be denied or abridged by the United States or by any State on account of sex.

SECTION 2. The Congress shall have the power to enforce, by appropriate legislation, the provisions of this article.

SECTION 3. This amendment shall take effect two years after the date of ratification.

INDEX

INDEX

References are to Pages

[*378*]

[*379*]

INDEX

INDEX

INDEX

INDEX
References are to Pages

[*385*]

INDEX

References are to Pages